SpringerBriefs in Psychology

Cognition

Series editor

Sandro Rubichi, University of Modena and Reggio Emilia, Modena, Italy

For further volumes:
http://www.springer.com/series/10737

Anna M. Borghi · Ferdinand Binkofski

Words as Social Tools: An Embodied View on Abstract Concepts

Springer

Anna M. Borghi
University of Bologna
Bologna
Italy

and

Institute of Cognitive Sciences
and Technologies
Italian National Research Council
Rome
Italy

Ferdinand Binkofski
RWTH Aachen University
Aachen
Germany

Even if this book was conceived by the two authors together, Ferdinand Binkofski has written and is the main responsible of Chapter 5, Anna Borghi has written and is the main responsible of the other chapters. Correspondence should be addressed to both authors.

ISSN 2192-8363 ISSN 2192-8371 (electronic)
ISBN 978-1-4614-9538-3 ISBN 978-1-4614-9539-0 (eBook)
DOI 10.1007/978-1-4614-9539-0
Springer New York Heidelberg Dordrecht London

Library of Congress Control Number: 2014932978

Printed on acid-free paper

Springer is part of Springer Science+Business Media (www.springer.com)

From Anna
To Lola, Luca and Francesco, with all my love, phantasy and energy. To my parents, Vanna and Gigi, with gratitude

From Ferdinand
To Bettina, Anja and Erik for their unlimited love and support. To Walter Huber, Walter Sturm and Klaus Willmes, who shaped the landscape of German Clinical Neuropsychology and with whom I had the honour and the pleasure to work and to share the common department

Acknowledgments

First of all, we would like to thank Sandro Rubichi for inviting us to write this book, to the editor for accepting our proposal, and to Martin Fischer for his accurate, extremely useful, and insightful work as reviewer. A special thank you to Irene Mittelberg for the many insightful comments and suggestions. Thanks also to Massimiliano Miatton, Felice Cimatti, Claudia Scorolli, and Carmen Granito, who read the manuscript and provided us with useful comments, and to Luca Tummolini for continuous discussions on the topic. Thanks to Olga Capirci, Gabriele Gianfreda, and Virginia Volterra for discussions and feedback on the sign language part. Thanks to Laura Barca, Cristina Burani, Cristiano Castelfranchi, Fabian Chersi, Federico Da Rold, Davide Marocco, Domenico Parisi, Giovanni Pezzulo, Lucia Riggio, and Corrado Roversi for stimulating discussions on abstract concepts and words. Thanks as well to all the members, present and past, of the EMbodied COgnition lab (http://www.emcolab.unibo.it). Thanks to all the people who, in different ways, supported us.

Contents

1 The Problem of Definition 1
- 1.1 Abstract Concepts and Word Meanings: How to Define Them? 1
- 1.2 Abstraction and Abstractness 3
  - 1.2.1 Abstractness and the Glue of Language 4
- 1.3 Some Hints from Psycholinguistics 7
  - 1.3.1 Concreteness Effect and Its Accounts 7
  - 1.3.2 Problems in Selecting Abstract Words: Perceptual Strength 8
  - 1.3.3 The Abstractness of Emotions 9
  - 1.3.4 The Problems Highlighted by Psycholinguistics 11
- 1.4 Abstract and Concrete Words: Dichotomy, Continuum or Other? 12
- 1.5 Conclusion: Definition is a Hard Job 14
- References 15

2 The WAT Proposal and the Role of Language 19
- 2.1 The WAT Proposal, in a Nutshell 19
- 2.2 Some Reasons Why Language is so Important for ACWs 22
- 2.3 What is Crucial in Language? Sounds, Labels, Explanations? 24
  - 2.3.1 Phonology 25
  - 2.3.2 Auditory Properties 26
  - 2.3.3 Labels 28
  - 2.3.4 Explanations 30
- 2.4 Which Mechanisms? 31
- 2.5 Conclusion: WAT and the Scaffolding Role of Language 34
- References 35

3 Embodied and Hybrid Theories of Abstract Concepts and Words 39
- 3.1 Introduction 39
- 3.2 Grounding in Action of both Concrete and Abstract Concepts 39

3.3 Differences in Content Between Concrete and Abstract Concepts . . . 43
3.3.1 Situations and Introspective Properties. . . . 44
3.3.2 Emotions . . . 46
3.4 Metaphors. . . . 47
3.5 Multiple Representation View . . . 51
3.5.1 Representational Pluralism: Dove . . . 52
3.5.2 Grounding and Sign Tracking: Jesse Prinz . . . 55
3.5.3 Hybrid Models: Distributional and Embodied Approaches . . . 57
3.6 Conclusions: Many Theories, One Unifying Theory? . . . 63
References . . . 64

4 Word Learning and Word Acquisition . . . 71
4.1 Introduction . . . 71
4.2 Social Aspects in Word Learning . . . 71
4.2.1 Cultural Psychology and Vygotsky . . . 72
4.2.2 Studies on Testimony . . . 73
4.2.3 Comparative Studies on Apes and Children . . . 75
4.3 Embodiment and Statistics in Word Learning . . . 77
4.4 Hybrid Approaches of Word Learning . . . 79
4.5 Age of Acquisition and Modality of Acquisition . . . 82
4.6 Acquisition of Novel Words in Adults: An Embodied Approach . . . 83
4.7 Conclusion: A Possible Acquisition Trajectory . . . 90
References . . . 91

5 What Can Neuroscience Tell Us About Abstract Concepts . . . 95
5.1 Concreteness Effect . . . 95
5.2 Reversed Concreteness Effect in Patients with Deep Dyslexia and Herpes Encephalitis . . . 96
5.3 Neuroimaging of Abstract and Concrete Concepts and Mental Imagery . . . 97
5.4 Neuroimaging of Abstract and Concrete Concepts and Emotional Valence . . . 102
5.5 Conclusion: Hints from Neuroscience . . . 104
References . . . 105

6 Language, Languages, and Abstract Concepts . . . 111
6.1 Introduction . . . 111
6.2 Abstract Concepts and Rich Linguistic Context: Computational Linguistics Evidence . . . 111

6.3 Abstract Concepts and Sign Language: Some Examples from Italian Sign Language 113
6.4 Abstract Concepts and Differences Between Languages 116
6.5 Conclusion: Influence of Language on Abstract Concepts 121
References 122

Afterword: A Short Story on Abstract Concepts 125

Index 127

Author Biography

Anna M. Borghi is an associate professor in Psychology at the University of Bologna; her research is conducted both at the Department of Psychology of the University of Bologna and at the Institute of Cognitive Sciences and Technologies, National Research Council in Rome, Italy. She has been a visiting scholar at various American universities (University of Chicago, University of Wisconsin-Madison, Emory University-Atlanta). She is Associate editor of the journal Frontiers in Cognition and of Psychological Research. She has just finished to coordinate the FP7 funded ROSSI (Emergence of Communication in Robots through Sensorimotor and Social Interaction) project. Her research themes include affordances, categorization, the relationships between concepts and perception and action, and between language and the motor system, abstract concepts.

Ferdinand Binkofski is professor and chairman for Cognitive Neurology at the RWTH Aachen University, he is also affiliated with the Institute for Neuroscience and Medicine at the Research Center Jülich. In Aachen he also heads study courses in speech and language pathology. Before his move to Aachen he was one of the managing directors of the Neuro Image Nord neuroimaging center of the north German universities of Hamburg, Kiel, and Lübeck. He has managed or is still managing several national and international research networks in behavioral and cognitive neuroscience. His research is dedicated to higher motor control and cognitive neurology. He is exploring the link between action and perception and between the language and the motor system.

Chapter 1
The Problem of Definition

There is no abstract art. You must always start with something. Afterward you can remove all traces of reality.

Picasso

I hardly need to abstract things, for each object is unreal enough already, so unreal that I can only make it real by means of painting.

Max Beckmann

1.1 Abstract Concepts and Word Meanings: How to Define Them?

This book is about abstract concepts and abstract word meanings. Humans have the amazing ability to distinguish objects and entities, forming categories—categories of prays and predators, of artefacts and living beings, of animals and plants. Concepts can be seen as the cognitive side of categories (Barsalou et al. 2003), a sort of "mental glue" that links our past with our current experiences in the world (Murphy 2002). Concepts are grounded in our sensory and motor system, that is they reactivate previous experiences with their referents, helping us to act in the environment in which we are immersed (Barsalou 1999; Borghi 2005; Gallese and Lakoff 2005). For example, possessing a concept of "ball" helps us predicting what to do when we see a novel ball. Once formed, many concepts are then typically associated with names. In this book we will equate concepts with word meanings. This might seem problematic. Word meanings are typically less broad and more constrained than the corresponding concepts, since language contributes in rendering the boundaries between categories more tight (Cangelosi and Parisi 1998; Cangelosi and Harnad 2000); in addition, there exist concepts without a clear linguistic counterpart. In this sense, even other animals besides humans can possess concepts. At the same time, however, it is possible that humans ability to categorize is influenced from the start by the important fact that we are a linguistic species. Furthermore, the influence of language is so pervasive and literature on human concepts is so influenced by studies on language that in most cases it is not possible to distinguish between concepts and word meanings. For these reasons, we will use the term "concepts" and the term "words" to refer to both concepts and word meanings, unless otherwise specified.

This book deals with the marvelous capacity humans have to form not only concrete but also abstract concepts, as well as to use abstract word meanings. As the quotes at the beginning of the chapter suggest, defining abstract concepts—as abstract art—is not an easy matter, and it is a controversial one. With abstract

A. M. Borghi and F. Binkofski, *Words as Social Tools: An Embodied View on Abstract Concepts*, SpringerBriefs in Cognition,
DOI: 10.1007/978-1-4614-9539-0_1, © The Author(s) 2014

concepts and word meanings we refer to concepts mediated by words as "freedom" and "truth". To clarify: we do not intend to claim that words are abstract. All words are material and perceivable—for example, they can be heard, pronounced or read. When we use the term "abstract words", in keeping with the literature, we refer to the fact that their meaning is abstract. There exist indeed words the referents of which are not material, perceivable, concrete objects and entities, as "balls" and "cats". Their referents are instead mental states, events, conditions, as "thought", "justice", "totalitarism". This book will deal with them. Notice that not all abstract concepts are abstract in the same way but that there might be different degrees of abstractness. As argued by Larry Barsalou (2003), concepts become increasingly abstract (e.g., from "pen" to "truth") as they become more detached from physical entities, and more associated with mental states.

Below we list the main characteristics that, in our view, characterize abstract concepts.

Different grounding Abstract concepts are not grounded in physical entities and in concrete, single objects, as concrete concepts. This does not imply at all that abstract concepts are not grounded or that their referents are not material, since they might be grounded in situations, events, mental states, and in complex relations between objects etc. Notice however that there is always a continuum between abstract and concrete concepts. Very concrete concepts have abstract aspects and vice versa. Consider for example the notion of "penny": it refers to a concrete, manipulable element, but it has some abstract properties, as the possibility to be exchanged, the value it is attached to it, etc. Furthermore, words that refer to concrete concepts can also have a metaphorical meaning, beyond the literal one. For example, we can speak of a mental "journey".

Complexity Abstract concepts are more complex than concrete ones. As argued by Larry Barsalou: "abstract concepts often capture complex configurations of physical and mental events" (Barsalou 2003, p. 1185), i.e. they evoke spatial, temporal and causal relations. This definition relies on data showing that abstract concepts evoke properties and relations more than objects and events (e.g., Wiemer-Hastings and Xu 2005).

Meaning variability Abstract concepts meaning is highly changeable compared to the meaning of concrete words. It is much easier to gain consensus on what "bottle" means and evoke, than on what "truth" means and evoke. In addition, an abstract concept such as "truth" is more exposed to the different experiences compared to a concept such as "bottle". This does not mean that "bottle" is a stable concept while truth is not, since both concepts are continuously updated and filled by new experiences with the category members. However, the meaning of abstract concepts is more variable and less stable, both across subjects and within the same subject.

So far we have introduced those that, in our opinion, are the main characteristics of abstract concepts and words. In the next paragraphs we will further deal with the problem of definition, trying to elucidate which concepts can be classified as abstract in our view. First, we will distinguish between superordinate concepts and abstract concepts, clarifying that this book does not focus on abstraction but rather on abstractness. A major part of the chapter is dedicated to the analysis of how psycholinguistic studies have addressed the problem of defining abstract concepts and words: we will describe the criteria that have been proposed to identify abstract words, and then we will discuss whether emotional terms can be considered as abstract or not. Finally we will discuss whether the distinction between concrete and abstract concepts can be considered as a dichotomy, as a continuum or whether more fine-grained analyses of the different kinds of abstract concepts are necessary.

1.2 Abstraction and Abstractness

A first question that might rise is the following: Would words as "animal" or as "artifact" be considered as abstract ones? Animals and artifacts might come in a great variety—foxes, robins and penguins do not have much in common, and neither do chairs and screwdrivers. In addition, the superordinate term "animal" is certainly more abstract than the basic term "dog", since it refers to a collection of rather diverse exemplars. But even the subordinate term "cocker" can be considered as partially abstract, since it abstracts and extracts some common characteristics from the experience of different cockers.

The definition we proposed might appear only as a negative one. It seems that we clarify what abstract concepts are NOT, not what they are. For these reasons, in order to answer to the question above and to provide a positive definition it is important to distinguish between abstraction and abstractness.

Abstraction is the process by means of which "knowledge of a specific category has been abstracted out of the buzzing and blooming confusion of experience" by forming a summative representation of that experience (Barsalou 2003: 389). This form of abstraction is at the core of every form of categorization, since it regards both concrete concepts, i.e. concepts endowed with perceivable referents, and abstract concepts. While forming each category, indeed, we somehow "abstract" from single instances and specific experiences. Even a subordinate-level category, such as "cocker", abstracts from single instances of dogs, and obviously superordinate level categories such as "animal" abstract more than concrete ones.

Abstractness is sometimes conflated with abstraction. However, we intend to keep abstraction and abstractness separate as much as possible, and this book will focus on the last one. An example will clarify the reasons of this choice. Concepts as "animal" and "furniture" (on top of the abstraction hierarchy) are more abstract than "dog" and "chair", but their category members are all concrete instances. Concepts as "freedom" and "phantasy", instead, are not abstract because they are on top on a conceptual hierarchy, but because their referent/s are not concrete objects or entities: they are not visible, manipulable or perceivable through any of our senses. This does not imply that they are not grounded in our sensorimotor system. Take for example the concept of "phantasy": it is grounded since it refers to a sparse collection of elements, as it evokes situations, events, and it likely elicits internal introspective states. A further difference that might exist between concepts on top of an abstraction hierarchy, such as "animal" or "vehicle", and abstract ones such as "freedom", concerns quantification: we can easily count animals and vehicles, while the amount of freedom or of truth might vary. This distinction based on the easiness of quantification is difficult to operationalize, and further research is needed in order to verify to what extent it applies to all subsets of abstract concepts (numbers, for example, are a kind of abstract concepts that can obviously be taken as quantifiable, even if they belong to a different symbolic system. However, we will see that numbers represent a special kind of abstract concepts).

One of the main reasons why we intend to focus on abstractness rather than on abstraction is a theoretical one. Explaining abstract concepts and words (abstractness) constitutes a major challenge for embodied and grounded theories of cognition (EGC) (Barsalou 1999, 2003, 2008; Borghi and Pecher 2011, 2012; Borghi and Caruana (in press); Gallese and Lakoff 2005; Myachykov et al. 2013). EGC theories assume that our bodily characteristics constrain our cognitive processes, from perception and action to processes traditionally considered as 'high level' processes such as language and thought. Many scientists nowadays recognize that these theories are rather powerful in explaining conceptual representation, as the burst of recent evidence on activation of perception and action while processing concrete concepts and words has shown. However, the number of skeptics is rather consistent when abstract concepts, such as "truth", "phantasy" and "justice", come into play. One of the aims of this book is to propose a theory of abstract concepts and words in keeping with an embodied and grounded perspective of cognition.

1.2.1 Abstractness and the Glue of Language

In this book we will propose and defend the view that, the more concepts increase in abstractness, the more they need some sort of glue that keeps the different category members together (Murphy 2002). This glue in our view is relevant for all concepts, but it becomes highly important for concepts on top of the abstraction hierarchy, as superordinate terms (e.g., "plants"), and it is particularly crucial for abstract concepts (e.g., "thought"). This also raises the question of whether abstract concepts have a prototypical and a hierarchical structure like concrete concepts (animal-dog-cocker). Probably they do not, because they are more a concept than a category with prototypical examples and superordinate and subordinate members.

Let us consider first concepts that do differ in abstraction but not in degree of abstractness, as subordinate and superordinate terms (e.g., "siamese cat", "animal"). The glue that keeps together different members of superordinate categories can be given by the presence of a common context where different category members can be found. Murphy and Wisniewski (1989) have demonstrated that

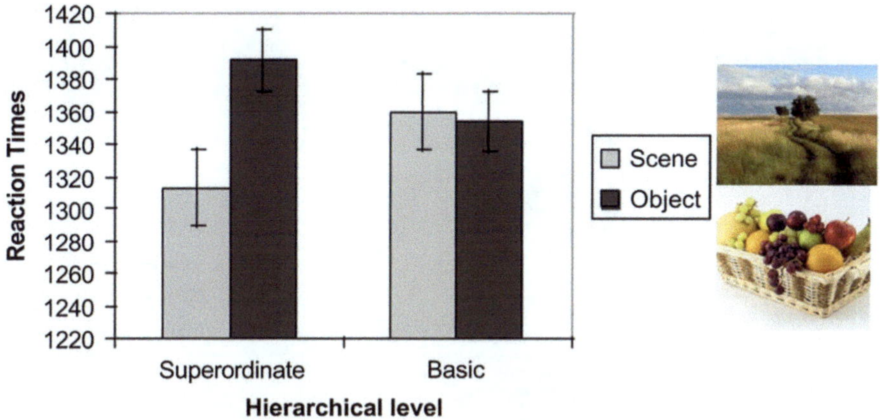

Fig. 1.1 Study by Borghi et al. (2005). The interaction between concepts and locations. In a location verification task with words superordinate concepts (e.g., fruit) yelded faster response times with broader locations (scenes) (e.g., countryside, for fruit/orange), which could contain more exemplars, while basic concepts (e.g., orange) yelded faster responses with object locations (e.g., basket, for fruit/orange). The result suggests that the context can be a sort of glue linking together different exemplars of a category

the role of context is more relevant for the recognition of superordinate concepts (e.g., "musical instruments") than of basic level ones (e.g., "guitar"). Participants were presented with a basic or superordinate category name, followed by a picture of a scene where the depicted objects could either fit in or not. Afterwards, a dot was presented in the same position as that in which there was an object in the scene; the task consisted in judging whether the cued object was a member of the named category or not. Inappropriate scenes affected participants' decision more often when the name referred to superordinate than to basic level concepts. Borghi et al.(2005) (see Fig. 1.1) have shown with both a location production task and asking participants to evaluate the adequacy of different contexts to the category members that superordinate concepts elicit broader contexts, where many category members can coexist. In a similar vein, Kalénine et al. (2009) found with a categorization task submitted to both children and adults that the advantage of basic level over superordinate level concepts was reduced when a target-image was preceded by a scene context rather than by an action priming context (see Fig. 1.2).

Overall, this evidence suggests that superordinate concepts are represented as a collection of exemplars, and a common context helps understanding their communalities. In contrast, the context is not so necessary to be able to recognize single instances of basic level categories, such as dogs or chairs.

One further powerful glue can be given by language. Having one common label helps keep together sparse situations, experiences, mental states. This is true for words of all hierarchical levels, from subordinate (e.g., "cocker") to superordinate level (e.g., "animal"), even if it is more crucial for more general terms, whose

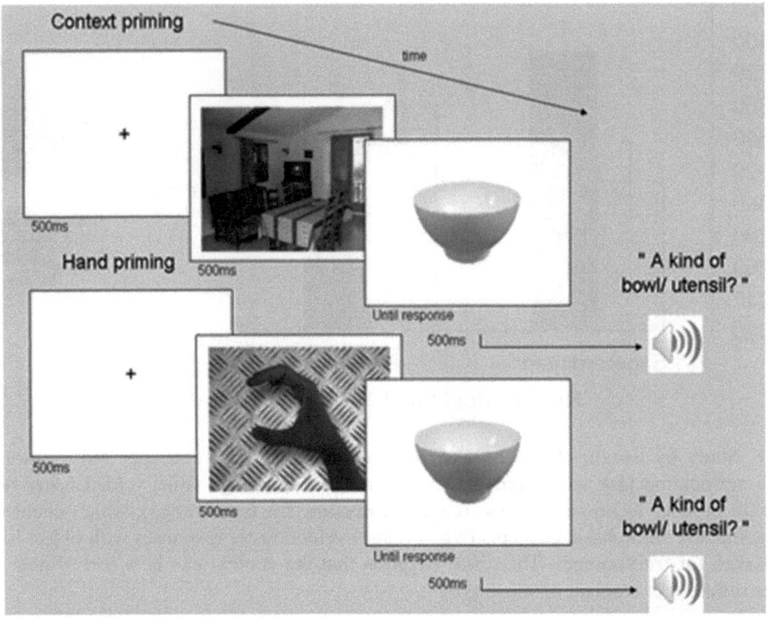

Fig. 1.2 Study by Kalénine et al. (2009). Children aged 7 and 9 and adults performed a categorization task with basic and superordinate terms following the form "a kind of…?" The target image was preceded by an action prime, consisting in a photograph of a hand in a grasping posture, or by a context prime, consisting in a photograph representing a scene. As it can be seen in the graph, irrespective of age results showed that the advantage of the basic-level task over the superordinate one was greater in the hand priming condition than in the context priming condition. This supports the idea that context works as a kind of glue linking together different exemplars of a category, and that this is true in particular for superordinate level concepts given the diversity of their category members

members are not characterized by high perceptual similarities. Similarly, such a glue is important for both concrete (e.g., "pen") and abstract words (e.g., "freedom"), even if having a common label is particularly important for abstract words.

To summarize: All concepts, even specific subordinate level ones, abstract to some extent from the single instances of the category: for example, a cocker is not our Fufi. However, having a common label is more crucial for general, superordinate level terms, which hold together a variety of different members: for example, "animal" includes cockers and other dogs, cats, birds, fishes, etc. And possessing a unifying label becomes critical for abstract terms, such as "truth", "knowledge" and "tolerance", since the exemplars of abstract concepts are even more sparse and diverse. The role language plays for abstractness will be further developed in the next chapters.

1.3 Some Hints from Psycholinguistics

A wide psycholinguistics literature has addressed the problem of concrete and abstract words representation. In this paragraph we will focus on this literature, in particular on how psycholinguists distinguish between concrete and abstract words. Referring to this kind of research helps us understand the difficulties in defining concrete and abstract concepts and in operationalizing the two constructs. At the same time, we are convinced that this literature can give us some hints and cues on how to interpret current evidence.

1.3.1 Concreteness Effect and Its Accounts

A difficult problem psycholinguistic studies had to address concerns the selection of abstract and concrete terms. Psycholinguistics researchers usually select and distinguish concrete and abstract words on the basis of ratings. For example, people are submitted to huge samples of words and are required to rate them on 7 point scales on a variety of dimensions. Aside from the more obvious dimension of concreteness, the typically used dimensions are imageability and context availability.

The choice of testing the dimensions of imageability and context availability in order to select abstract words is due to theoretical reasons. Two of the most influential explanations of the so-called "concreteness effect" rely indeed on imageability and on contextual availability. The "concreteness effect" consists in the processing advantage and best recall of concrete over abstract words (Schwanenflugel et al. 1988; Schwanenflugel and Shoben 1983; Schwanenflugel and Stowe 1989); this effect is rather consistent: it was found in both children and adults, and in a variety of tasks, such as lexical decision, free recall, recognition, and language comprehension (for a brief review see Altarriba and Bauer 2004; Altarriba et al. 1999). However, there is some controversy since some studies have not found evidence of concreteness effects (e.g., Barca et al. 2002) and an advantage in processing of abstract over concrete concepts has been reported as well, both by Kousta et al. (2011) and Barber et al. (2013), who controlled for items valence, and by Pexman et al. (2007) in an edible/non edible categorization task.

According to the classical Contextual Availability Theory (CAT; Schwanenflugel et al. 1988, 1992), while concrete concepts and words are strongly associated to a reduced numbers of contexts, abstract concepts and words are only weakly associated to a higher number of contexts. Hence, when words are presented in isolation, contextual information is more easily accessible for concrete than for abstract words. This determines the worse recall of abstract compared to concrete words.

This theory has not been confirmed by some recent evidence. For example, it has been shown that imageability and contextual relatedness influence memory tasks in an independent fashion, not in an integrated way, as the CAT would predict.

The concreteness effect is ascribed to a different cause by Paivio's (1986) dual coding theory (DCT). According to DCT, concrete and abstract words are encoded in two functionally related systems. While concrete words are coded both in an imagery and in a verbal system, abstract words are encoded only verbally. Hence, abstract word meanings can be imagined only indirectly, through the mediation of associated concrete words. For example, while the concrete concept "bottle" can be directly imagined, the abstract concept of "religion"can be imagined only through concrete images such as that of "church" (maybe also "praying", "worship", etc.). The necessity of the mediation would slow down processing of abstract words and would thus lead to the concreteness effect. Notice however that, as recently argued by Paivio (2013), depending on the stimuli and on the task even the reverse of the concreteness effect can be predicted by DCT. Furthermore, notice that in the DCT theory abstract words are not defined in terms of what they are but rather in terms of what they lack compared to concrete words (for a similar critique, see Vigliocco et al. 2013).

1.3.2 Problems in Selecting Abstract Words: Perceptual Strength

As we have seen, the dimensions which are typically used in order to select abstract terms are imageability, context availability and concreteness. However, it is not always the case that all these dimensions are tested. Furthermore, even if all these dimensions are taken into account, they might not be able to fully explain what laypeople intend with concrete and abstract words. We will address the two issues separately.

One downside of much current evidence is that in many cases abstract terms are selected solely on the basis of imageability ratings and not of concreteness ratings: the two dimensions of imageability and concreteness have often been conflated without considering eventual distinctions between them (e.g., Nelson and Schreiber 1992; Binder et al. 2005; Sabsevitz et al. 2005). This choice is disputable since the two kinds of ratings are correlated, but not identical. Even if Paivio (2013) argues that "they are so highly correlated that for most research purposes they can be used interchangeably" (p. 283); still, they are not the same, and concreteness ratings are characterized by a higher variability compared to imageability ratings. According to Kousta et al. (2009, 2011), imageability ratings explain 72 % of the variance in concreteness ratings. Their distribution differs as well: looking at the ratings for more than 4,000 words in the MRC Psycholinguistic Database, Kousta et al. (2009) report that, while concreteness is characterized by a bimodal distribution (i.e. by the opposition between concrete and abstract words), imageability has an unimodal distribution.

The second limit of the usual way to select abstract and concrete words is that, even when considered together, imageability, concreteness and contextual availability do not fully account for what people normally intend with concrete and abstract words (Connell and Lynott 2012). This is likely due to some problems in ratings collection. Consider for example imageability ratings. Instructions for imageability ratings refer to arousing mental images (Paivio et al. 1968, p. 4). This choice is biased, as it might induce participants to focus on vision at the expenses of other sensory modalities, as recently shown by Connell and Lynott (2012). To avoid the visual bias characterizing imageability ratings, Lynott and Connell (2009) collected norms asking subjects to evaluate, together with imageability and concreteness, perceptual strength according to the different sensory modalities: auditory, gustatory, haptic, olfactory and visual. Concrete words ratings were predicted by olfactory and visual strength; abstract words ratings were positively related to vision and negatively to auditory and olfactory strength. Other sensory modalities did not play any role. In general, concreteness variance was explained for 19 % in concrete words and for 8 % in abstract words by perceptual strength; this indicates that concrete concepts rely more than abstract ones on perceptual aspects, but at the same time it questions the use of concreteness and of imageability as dimensions to be used to select concrete and abstract concepts. Consistently with this, Lynott and Connell (2009) showed that variance in RTs and accuracy in lexical decision and word naming tasks were predicted by perceptual strength more than by concreteness and imageability.

To sum up: some recent studies (e.g., Kousta et al. 2009) indicate that imageability and concreteness norms shouldn't be conflated, as it was done in a variety of studies, since these two dimensions are correlated but different. This invites us to be very cautious in interpreting and comparing the results in the literature. In addition, Lynott and Connell (2009, 2013), Connell and Lynott (2012) have recently shown that concreteness effects are predicted more by perceptual strength than by concreteness/imageability norms. Thus, norms of concreteness and imageability do not seem to fully capture the perceptual dimension of concepts. And it is a fact that, the more perceptually grounded concepts are, the faster they are processed. The discovery that concreteness/imageability norms do not account for what people normally intend with concrete and abstract words has some consequences. At a minimum, it invites us to take with caution all experimental results, since the selection of concrete versus abstract terms is often based on ratings that do not fully capture their gist and their differences.

1.3.3 The Abstractness of Emotions

One further problem psycholinguistic research has addressed, concerns whether emotional terms can be considered as abstract or not. Can words as "love" and "rage" be considered as abstract ones? The issue is quite complicated. Consider for example "rage". Differently from "phantasy", "rage" can be experienced, either perceived through our senses or recognized in others' expressions—emotions have indeed a clear bodily counterpart. In our view, the choice to include emotional terms among the abstract ones is not really straightforward, for both empirical and theoretical reasons.

From an empirical point of view, evidence shows that ratings of abstract and emotional terms differ along various dimensions. Altarriba et al. (1999) collected concreteness, imageability and context availability ratings for concrete, abstract and emotional words. They showed that on scales on concreteness and context availability emotive words ratings were lower compared to ratings of concrete and abstract words, while they were rated higher on imageability. While Nelson and Schreiber (1992) had found no correlation between imageability and context availability (but used a sample composed by emotional terms and abstract ones), Altarriba et al. (1999) demonstrated for the first time the existence of positive correlations between context availability and concreteness. More crucially for us, the correlations between these two dimensions and imageability were not significant for concrete and emotional terms, while they were significant for abstract words. This result testifies that emotional words differ from abstract words, even if often in the literature emotional words are included within the sample of abstract ones. This difference was maintained also when asking participants to write an associate word to the 3 kinds of terms: Altarriba et al. (1999) found that the highest number of associations were elicited by emotional words, followed by abstract and then by concrete words (Given that the larger is the number of paths associated to a word, the more difficult is to retrieve information from each path, this results pattern can lead to the prediction that retrieval would be more easy for concrete, then for abstract, then for emotional concepts.).

Further theoretical reasons might induce researchers to keep abstract and emotional terms apart. Emotional terms evoke emotional states and bodily experiences: differently from abstract concepts such as "truth", they are directly grounded in bodily experiences. These experiences, though variable, have some constancy across situations and events. These two characteristics differ from those that in our opinion are the most fundamental characteristics of abstract concepts, i.e. the difficulty in grounding, as well as the inter-subjective and within-subject variability of meaning (see Sect. 1.1). High-level and more complex emotional concepts, such as "envy", might be closer to standard abstract concepts such as "truth" than more basic other emotional terms, such as "anger" or the other emotions considered as basic, as disgust, fear, happiness, sadness, and surprise.

Even if considering emotional terms as abstract might seem problematic, many studies on abstract concepts and words do include emotional concepts among abstract ones, sometimes for the simple reason that people do rate them as abstract. In particular, one recent and influential theory proposes that abstract terms are more emotionally connoted than concrete ones. Analyzing a large database Kousta et al. (2009, 2011) demonstrated that, when imageability was held constant, valence was a significant predictor of concreteness ratings: the more emotionally connoted a word was, the more abstract it was rated. In addition, positive words were rated as more abstract than negative ones. Crucially, once imageability and context availability were kept constant, the usual "concreteness effect" disappeared and was substituted by an opposite "abstractness effect", due to the influence of emotional content/valence. According to Kousta et al. (2009, 2011), these results indicate that emotional content strongly characterizes the way in which abstract terms are represented (see Chap. 3 for a deeper analysis of this issue).

To summarize: psycholinguistic literature gives us some important hints, which indicate that deciding whether to consider emotional concepts as abstract ones or not can seriously impact results. This invites us to be cautious in analyzing the empirical results obtained in the literature. The choice to include or not emotional terms within abstract ones depends also from the explanation adopted, of the difference between concrete and abstract concepts. If a dichotomic account is adopted, according to which concrete and abstract concepts are considered as opposite to each other, then emotional terms could be included within abstract concepts, since both emotional and abstract concepts do not refer to concrete, manipulable objects. If, instead, the idea of a continuum between concrete and abstract concepts is adopted, then emotional concepts could be considered as a sub-domain the members of which are more abstract than concrete terms but less abstract than standard abstract concepts, as "truth". As we will see in Sect. 1.4, we do not favour a dychotomic account.

1.3.4 The Problems Highlighted by Psycholinguistics

Defining abstract concepts and words is not an easy matter. As we have seen, the attempts made in psycholinguistics to operationalize the distinction between concrete and abstract words, even if really useful, incur in a number of problems, which invite to be cautious in taking current results for granted.

The first problem is due to the tendency to conflate imageability and concreteness, while the two dimensions are correlated but differ. The second concerns the contradictory results obtained in the literature: typically imageability and concreteness are not positively correlated to context availability, but according to some studies they are. The third problem concerns the fact that recent evidence indicates that perceptual strength rather than concreteness and imageability predict concreteness effects. One further problem concerns the role played by emotional terms—Altarriba et al. have shown that emotional and standard abstract concepts have different characteristics, while the majority of literature includes them within abstract concepts, and a recent theory proposes that emotional valence is the hallmark of abstractness.

Overall, the difficulties we addressed in operationalizing abstract concepts cast some doubts on the possibility to interpret in an unambiguous and constant way evidence in the field. The criteria used to select abstract concepts can indeed be based on different kinds of ratings (for example concreteness or imageability), and in some cases emotional and abstract concepts are assimilated, while in other cases they are not. As we have seen, depending on the criteria selection the concreteness effect could be present or even reversed. In general, this brief analysis clarifies that the data collected sometimes rely on different definitions of abstract concepts, hence they are selected on the basis of different criteria. This renders it quite difficult to interpret experimental results in a cumulative fashion.

1.4 Abstract and Concrete Words: Dichotomy, Continuum or Other?

As we have seen scrutinizing in a synthetic way psycolinguistics literature, operationalizing the distinction between concrete and abstract words is not an easy task.

The majority of psycholinguistic studies have differentiated concrete and abstract terms, considering abstract concepts and words as dichotomically opposed to concrete concepts and words. While according to the majority of the studies the distinction is more quantitative than qualitative, on the basis of work with patients some authors have proposed that they are characterized by qualitatively different principles of organization: concrete concepts and words would mostly rely on categorical similarity, abstract concepts and words on semantic associations (e.g., Crutch and Warrington 2005 on semantic refractory access dysphasia; Duñabeitia et al. 2009; see Marques and Nunes 2012, for a different view, according to which the organization principle underlying associations to concrete and abstract concepts does not differ) (see Chap. 5 for a thorough analysis).

A different, to us more plausible view maintains that there is no concrete-abstract dichotomy; the distinction between concrete and abstract concepts can instead be seen as a continuum going from very abstract concepts and words, as "democracy", to very concrete ones, such as "chair" (Wiemer-Hastings et al. 2001), with a progressive detachment from physical experiences (Barsalou 2003). A similar view was proposed some years ago by Keil (1989), according to whom concepts are arranged along a continuum. At one extreme of this continuum there are pure natural kind concepts (e.g., "dog"), followed by complex artifacts (e.g., "train"), by simple artifacts (e.g., "hammer"), and then by nominal concepts of the social role category (e.g., "teacher"). At the other extreme there are pure nominal concepts, the content of which is established by definition, like "odd number". While the first kinds of concepts can be considered as concrete ones, the two last ones are more easily accomodated within the domain of abstract concepts.

The idea of continuum with abstractness and concreteness at the two opposite ends is intuitively appealing and supported by the fact that concrete and abstract words seem to have a bipolar distribution (Wiemer-Hastings et al. 2001; Kousta et al. 2009). However, even the assumption of a continuum can be challenged by contrasting experimental data. For example, analyzing perceptual strength Connell and Lynott (2012) found that more olfactory meant both more abstract and more concrete. This result is possibly due to the fact that participants did not respect the instructions requiring them to consider any sensory experience as a concreteness hallmark: vision played for them a major role, while the other sensory modalities

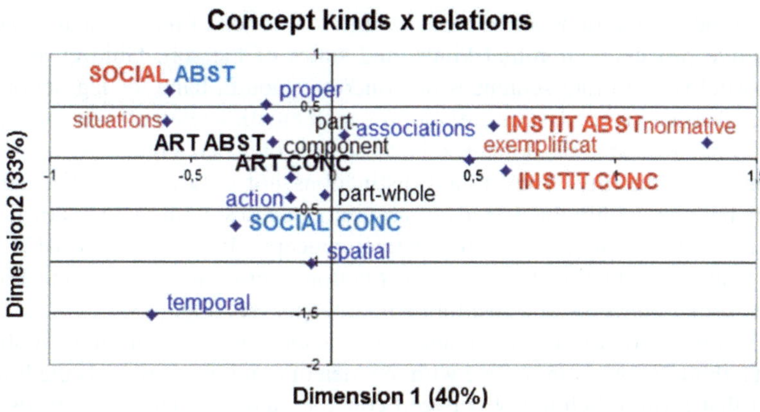

Fig. 1.3 Study by Roversi et al. (2013). The correspondence analysis between the four concept kinds and the relations they elicited. The concept kinds are: concrete standard artefacts (e.g., screwdriver); abstract standard artefacts (e.g., project); concrete institutional artefacts (e.g., check); abstract institutional artefacts (e.g., ownership); concrete social entities (e.g., party); abstract social entities (e.g., friendship). The two dimensions are highlighted in the graph with the colors blue and red. As it can be seen in the graph, Dimension 1 (40 % of the variance) shows the opposition between concrete and abstract institutional artefacts, characterized by exemplifications and normative relations, which differ from abstract social entities characterized by situations. To notice that the relevance of exemplifications and normative relations for institutional artefacts holds for both abstract or concrete concepts, while the relevance of situational relations for social concepts in opposition to institutional artefacts is specifically connected to abstract and not to concrete social concepts. Dimension 2 (33 % of the variance) is characterized by the opposition between concrete social entities, characterized by action, spatial and temporal relations, and abstract social entities, which elicit mental associations more often

were misconstrued, so that when something could be heard and smelled but not seen, they rated it as abstract. Independently of the possible reasons underlying this result, its inconsistency poses serious problems to the idea of continuum.

A third alternative that is gaining more and more success in the recent literature consists in analysing different subsets of abstract concepts. Abstract concepts have indeed typically been considered as an unitary block, in contrast with concrete concepts, where categorical distinctions have been investigated in many behavioral, brain imaging and neuropsychological studies—one pivotal example is given by the opposition between artifacts and natural objects, or living and not living kinds (e.g., Humphreys and Forde 2001). However, recent work shows that there might be fine-grained distinctions among different types of abstract concepts. Using a definition task with children aged 9, 11, and 13, Caramelli et al. (2006) analysed differences within different kinds of nominal kind terms, i.e. pure nominal kinds, social role concepts, emotion concepts, time concepts and abstract concepts. Setti and Caramelli (2005) found with a definition production task that different kinds of relations are elicited by different kinds of mental state concepts, as cognitive processes, nominal kinds, and states of the self. Ghio et al. (2013) asked participants to rate sentences on concrete (mouth, hand, or leg action-related) and abstract (mental state-, emotion-, mathematics-related) categories, with respect either to semantic domain-related scales, or to concreteness, familiarity, and context availability. They found distinctions not only between the concrete concepts but also within the 3 kinds of abstract concepts, with mathematical terms considered in between concrete and abstract concepts. Roversi et al. (2013) found with a feature production task clear distinctions between concrete and abstract artifacts, social concepts and institutional concepts (see Fig. 1.3).

The identification of different nuances characterizing different kinds of abstract concepts, though not incompatible with the idea of continuum, reveals the limits of the idea that a rigid dichotomy between concrete and abstract words exists.

1.5 Conclusion: Definition is a Hard Job

In this chapter we have illustrated those that, in our view, are the main characteristics of abstract concepts. Compared to concrete concepts, abstract concepts are differently grounded; furthermore they are more complex, since they typically do not refer to single objects but rather to relations of entities, events, situations, and they are more variable, both within and across subjects. These criteria allowed us to delimit the focus of our analysis: we have distinguished between abstraction and abstractness, and have clarified that this book will focus on the second. We have also suggested that, the more concepts are abstract, the more they need some sort of glue that keeps their members together—and language can represent such a glue.

We then performed an analysis of the psycholinguistics literature with the aim to comprehend how abstract concepts were usually defined and selected. This analysis revealed that there is not a single unitary criterion which has been consistently used to select abstract concepts. This reflects the complexity of the topic but also invites us to a great caution in analysing and comparing current experimental results, since they might rely on concepts selected on the basis of different criteria.

In the course of the chapter, we have seen that the domain of abstract concepts is not as unitary and cohesive as it may appear. Different kinds of abstract concepts exist, and their degree of abstractness might vary. These differences render it difficult, to accept the idea of a dychotomic opposition between concrete and abstract words and leads us to favour the assumption that a continuum between concreteness and abstractness exist. The differences between abstract concepts and their variability explain at least in part the difficulty to define them as well as to find a unitary and comprehensive theory of abstractness, as we will see in the next chapters.

References

Altarriba, J., & Bauer, L. M. (2004). The distinctiveness of emotion concepts: a comparison between emotion, abstract, and concrete words. *American Journal of Psychology, 117*, 389–410. doi:10.2307/4149007

Altarriba, J., Bauer, L. M., & Benvenuto, C. (1999). Concreteness, context availability, and imageability ratings and word associations for abstract, concrete, and emotion words. *Behavior Research Methods, 31*, 578–602.

Barber, H. A., Otten, L. J., Kousta, S. T., & Vigliocco, G. (2013). Concreteness in word processing: ERP and behavioral effects in a lexical decision task. *Brain and Language, 125*(1), 47–53.

Barca, L., Burani, C., & Arduino, L. S. (2002). Word naming times and psycholinguistic norms for Italian nouns. *Behavior Research Methods, Instruments, and Computers, 34*, 424–434.

Barsalou, L. W. (1999). Perceptual symbol systems. *Brain and Behavioural Sciences, 22*, 577–660.

Barsalou, L. W. (2003). Abstraction in perceptual symbol systems. *Philosophical Transactions of the Royal Society of London: Biological Sciences, 358*, 1177–1187.

Barsalou, L. W. (2008). Grounded cognition. *Annual Review of Psychology, 59*, 617–645.

Barsalou, L. W., Simmons, W. K., Barbey, A. K., & Wilson, C. D. (2003). Grounding conceptual knowledge in modality-specific systems. *Trends in Cognitive Science, 7*, 84–91.

Binder, J. R., Westbury, C. F., McKiernan, K. A., Possing, E. T., & Medler, D. A. (2005). Distinct brain systems for processing concrete and abstract concepts. *Journal of Cognitive Neuroscience, 17*, 905–917. doi:10.1162/0898929054021102

Borghi, A. M. (2005). Object concepts and action. In D. Pecher & R. A. Zwaan (Eds.), *Grounding cognition: The role of perception and action in memory, language, and thinking* (pp. 8–34). Cambridge: Cambridge University Press.

Borghi, A. M., Caramelli, N., & Setti, A. (2005). Conceptual information on objects' locations. *Brain and Language, 93*, 140–151.

Borghi, A. M., & Caruana, F. (in press). Embodiment theories. In J. Wright (Ed.), *International encyclopedia of the social and behavioral sciences* (2nd ed.). (S. Cappa (Ed.), Section of cognitive neuroscience).

Borghi, A. M., & Pecher, D. (2011). Introduction to the special topic embodied and grounded cognition. *Frontiers in Psychology, 2*, 187. doi:10.3389/fpsyg.2011.00187

Borghi, A. M., & Pecher, D. (2012). *Special topic on embodied and grounded cognition.* Lousanne: Frontiers.

Cangelosi, A., & Harnad, S. (2000). The adaptive advantage of symbolic theft over sensorimotor toil: Grounding language in perceptual categories. *Evolution of Communication, 4*(1), 117–142.

Cangelosi, A., & Parisi, D. (1998). The emergence of a "language" in an evolving population of neural networks. *Connection Science, 10*, 83–97.

Caramelli, N., Borghi, A. M., & Setti, A. (2006). The identification of definition strategies in children of different ages. *Linguistica Computazionale, 26*, 155–177.

Connell, L., & Lynott, D. (2012). Strength of perceptual experience predicts word processing performance better than concreteness or imageability. *Cognition, 125*(3), 452–465.

Crutch, S. J., & Warrington, E. K. (2005). Abstract and concrete concepts have structurally different representational framework. *Brain, 128*, 615–627.

Duñabeitia, J. A., Avilés, A., Afonso, O., Scheepers, C., & Carreiras, M. (2009). Qualitative differences in the representation of abstract versus concrete words: Evidence from the visual-world paradigm. *Cognition, 110*, 284–292.

Gallese, V., & Lakoff, G. (2005). The brain's concepts: the role of the sensory-motor system in conceptual knowledge. *Cognitive Neuropsychology, 22*, 455–479.

Ghio, M., Vaghi, M. M. S., & Tettamanti, M. (2013). Fine-grained semantic categorization across the abstract and concrete domains. *PLoS ONE, 8*(6), e67090. doi:10.1371/journal.pone.0067090

Humphreys, G. W., & Forde, E. M. (2001). Hierarchies, similarity, and interactivity in object recognition: "category-specific" neuropsychological deficits. *Behavioral and Brain Sciences, 24*(3), 453–476. (discussion 476–509).

Kalénine, S., Bonthoux, F., & Borghi, A. M. (2009). How action and context priming influence categorization: a developmental study. *British Journal of Developmental Psychology, 27*, 717–730.

Keil, F. C. (1989). *Concepts, kinds and cognitive development*. London: MIT Press.

Kousta, S., Vigliocco, G., Vinson, D. P., & Andrews, M. (2009). Happiness is… an abstract word. The role of affect in abstract knowledge representation. In N. Taatgen & H. van Rijn (Eds.), *Proceedings of the 31st Annual Conference of the Cognitive Science Society*. Amsterdam: Cognitive Science Society.

Kousta, S. T., Vigliocco, G., Vinson, D. P., Andrews, M., & Del Campo, E. (2011). The representation of abstract words: Why emotion matters. *Journal of Experimental Psychology: General, 140*, 14–34.

Lynott, D., & Connell, L. (2009). Modality exclusivity norms for 423 object properties. *Behavior Research Methods, 41*, 558–564. doi:10.3758/BRM.41.2.558. (eScholarID:1d19006).

Lynott, D., & Connell, L. (2013). Modality exclusivity norms for 400 nouns: The relationship between perceptual experience and surface word form. *Behavior Research Methods, 45*(2), 516–526. doi:10.3758/s13428-012-0267-0. (eScholarID:171330).

Marques, F. J., & Nunes, L. D. (2012). The contribution of language and experience to the representation of abstract and concrete words: different weights but similar organization. *Memory and Cognition, 40*(8), 1266–1275.

Murphy, G. L. (2002). *The big book of concepts*. Cambridge: MIT.

Murphy, G. L., & Wisniewski, E. J. (1989). Categorizing objects in isolation and in scenes: What a superordinate is good for. *Journal of Experimental Psychology. Learning, Memory, and Cognition, 15*, 572–586.

Myachykov, A., Scheepers, C., Fischer, M. H., & Kessler, K. (2013). TEST: A tropic, embodied, and situated theory of cognition. *Topics in Cognitive Science, 5*, 1–19. doi:10.1111/tops.12024

Nelson, D. L., & Schreiber, T. A. (1992). Word concreteness and word structure as independent determinants of recall. *Journal of Memory and Language, 31*, 237–260. doi:10.1016/0749-596X(92)90013-N

Paivio, A. (1986). *Mental representations: A dual coding approach*. New York: Oxford University.

Paivio, A. (2013). Dual coding theory, word abstractness, and emotion: a critical review of Kousta et al. (2011). *Journal of Experimental Psychology: General, 142*(1), 282–287. doi:10.1037/a0027004

Paivio, A., Yuille, J. C., & Madigan, S. A. (1968). Concreteness, imagery, and meaningfulness values for 925 nouns. *Journal of Experimental Psychology, 76*(1, Pt.2), 1–25.

Pexman, P. M., Hargreaves, I. S., Edwards, J. D., Henry, L. C., & Goodyear, B. G. (2007). Neural correlates of concreteness in semantic categorization. *Journal of Cognitive Neuroscience, 19*, 1407–1419.

Roversi, C., Borghi, A. M., & Tummolini, L. (2013). A marriage is an artefact and not a walk that we take together: An experimental study on the categorization of artefacts. *Review of Philosophy and Psychology, 4*(3), 527–542.

Sabsevitz, D. S., Medler, D. A., Seidenberg, M., & Binder, J. R. (2005). Modulation of the semantic system by word imageability. *Neuroimage, 27*, 188–200. doi:10.1016/j.neuroimage.2005.04.012

Schwanenflugel, P. J., Akin, C., & Luh, W. M. (1992). Context availability and the recall of abstract and concrete words. *Memory and Cognition, 20*, 96–104.

Schwanenflugel, P. J., Harnishfeger, K. K., & Stowe, R. W. (1988). Context availability and lexical decisions for abstract and concrete words. *Journal of Memory and Language, 27*, 499–520. doi:10.1016/0749-596X(88)90022-8

Schwanenflugel, P. J., & Shoben, E. J. (1983). Differential context effects in the comprehension of abstract and concrete verbal materials. *Journal of Experimental Psychology. Learning, Memory, and Cognition, 9*, 82–102. doi:10.1037/0278-7393.9.1.82

Schwanenflugel, P. J., & Stowe, R. W. (1989). Context availability and the processing of abstract and concrete words in sentences. *Reading Research Quarterly, 24*, 114–126. doi:10.2307/748013

Setti A, & Caramelli, N. (2005) Different domains in abstract concepts. In B. Bara, L. Barsalou, & M. Bucciarelli (Eds.), *Proceedings of the XXVII Annual Conference of the Cognitive Science.* Mahwah, NJ: Erlbaum.

Vigliocco, G., Kousta, S., Vinson, D., Andrew, M., & Del Campo, E. (2013). The representation of abstract words: what matters? Reply to Paivio's (2013) comment on Kousta et al. (2011). *Journal of Experimental Psychology: General, 142*(1), 288–291. doi:10.1037/a0028749

Wiemer-Hastings, K., Krug, J., & Xu, X. (2001). Imagery, context availability, contextual constraints and abstractness. In *Proceedings of the 23rd Annual Meeting of the Cognitive Science Society* (pp. 1106–1111). Hillsdale, NJ: Erlbaum.

Wiemer-Hastings, K., & Xu, X. (2005). Content differences for abstract and concrete concepts. *Cognitive Science, 29*, 719–727.

Chapter 2
The WAT Proposal and the Role of Language

> *You learned the concept "pain" when you learned language. For a large class of cases—though not for all—in which we employ the word meaning, it can be explained thus: The meaning of a word is its use in the language.*
> *Every explanation is after all an hypothesis.*
>
> Ludwig Wittgenstein

2.1 The WAT Proposal, in a Nutshell

In this book, we intend to outline a theory which is able to account how different kinds of abstract concepts and words are represented. The theory is called WAT, an acronym for words as social tools (the initial formulation of this view was presented in Borghi and Cimatti 2009). Words can be seen as tools because, similar to physical tools, they allow us to act in the world, together with and in relation to other individuals; they are social also since they are acquired and used in a social context. We will claim that intending words as social tools will allow us to explain the representation in the brain of abstract concepts and word meanings (ACWs) and their use. As we have seen, abstract concepts come in a great variety, and we will argue that one of the problems of the theories proposed so far concerns their difficulty in providing a framework which is sufficiently general to deal with different kinds of abstract concepts.

The WAT theory we propose has five main tenets.

1. Embodiment and grounding of ACWs. First, we assume that not only concrete concepts and words but also ACWs are embodied and grounded in our perception, action, and emotional systems. This means that not only concrete words as "ball" but also words such as "truth" reactivate sensorimotor networks in the brain. As we will see in the next chapter, a variety of theories share this assumption, supported by growing evidence.
2. Importance of language for ACWs. The theory holds that for the representation of ACWs, the linguistic mediation is more crucial than for the representation of concrete concepts and words. This means that ACWs activate linguistic areas in the brain more than concrete concepts and words. Some embodied theories share this assumption, but the reasons advanced for this relevance of language may differ. We argue that language is more important for the representation of abstract

A. M. Borghi and F. Binkofski, *Words as Social Tools: An Embodied View on Abstract Concepts*, SpringerBriefs in Cognition,
DOI: 10.1007/978-1-4614-9539-0_2,

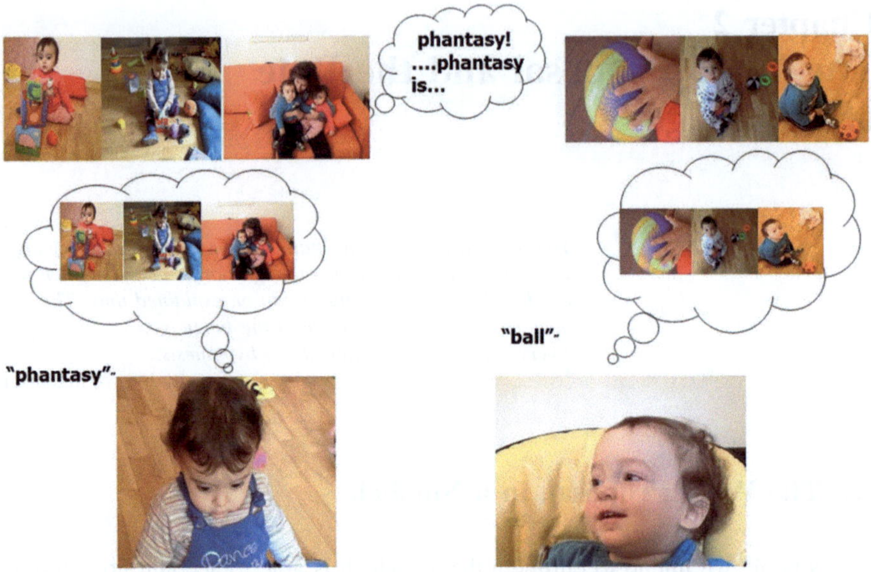

Fig. 2.1 The acquisition modality of concrete versus abstract words. The figure illustrates the tenet on acquisition of the WAT proposal: It shows that in order to learn a concrete concept such as "ball," the social input is less relevant than in order to learn the abstract concept "phantasy," which assembles many different experiences and states

than of concrete word meanings for at least two reasons. First, members of ACWs differ more than members of concrete concepts and words—for example, experiences of freedom differ more than experiences of balls—and are often more complex; thus, a unifying label can work as a glue (see Chap. 1). Second, due to the fact that they do not have concrete referents, the mediation of language might be more crucial for the acquisition of ACWs than of concrete concepts and words. We will develop this aspect in point 3; in the next chapters, we will present behavioral and neural data in keeping with this hypothesis.

3. Acquisition modality of ACWs (see Fig. 2.1). Given that ACWs do not have concrete referents, their acquisition modality relies more on language than the acquisition of concrete concepts and words. Take for example "ball" or "bottle": Infants can learn to differentiate bottles from glasses on the basis of their perceptual and motor experience. The presence of somebody using the same label indicating bottles and a different label indicating glasses certainly changes categorization: It helps to better differentiate between categories and it renders them more compact and cohese (Cangelosi and Parisi 1998; Lupyan 2012; Yoshida and Smith 2005). However, it is probably not necessary to form them. But consider now "freedom" and "democracy." The presence of somebody helping us, thanks to the use of the same label, to assemble and put together sparse and variable experiences, as those related to freedom, might be crucial. The presence of an authoritative member of our community telling us what democracy is can be crucial for the acquisition of the notion. This

authoritative member can be for example a parent, an expert, or a teacher. Literacy and schooling are obviously important to build up complexity around abstract concept skeleton, as it is independent reading of sources we trust. To clarify, concrete concepts still need tokens or labels. But, of course, those labels can be directly linked with the referent, a real object. For example, they can be pronounced in presence of it and the object can be indicated. Abstract words referent typically cannot be indicated. This does not imply that abstract concepts such as "freedom" are not grounded: Activating them, we probably reactivate previous experiences, visualize scenes, etc. But this visualization is probably not sufficient to create a category that keeps together the Statue of Freedom, the experience of running on a field, that of exiting prison, and many others, without the support of other people and the help of the linguistic mediation. With linguistic mediation, we do not intend exclusively the fact of using a given label in presence of an entity/event/situation, but also the fact that our conspecifics can provide us with explanations and meaning clarifications, and that in certain cases, we might need to have an idea of the social stratification of our in-group, to know the authoritative members of our community on whose opinion we intend to rely upon (Prinz 2002, 2012). To our knowledge, our theory is the unique, or the first, to propose this principle in combination with an embodied approach. In the next chapters, we will present some data on acquisition in adults and on conceptual development in children that support this hypothesis.

4. Brain representation of ACWs: We hypothesize that the different acquisition modality of concrete and abstract concepts and words is reflected in the way in which they are represented in the brain. While both should activate the sensorimotor network, the linguistic network should be activated more by the ACWs than by concrete concepts and words. In the next chapters, we will present some data in support of this.
5. Linguistic diversity of ACWs: Due to the fact that language plays a major role in the representation of ACWs, we hypothesize that they are more affected by differences between languages than concrete concepts and words, that is, that their meaning will change more depending on the cultural and linguistic milieu in which they are learned. This means that behavioral studies should show a higher variability in meaning of ACWs and a higher dependence of their meaning from the spoken (and written) language, compared to concrete concepts and words. In the next chapters, we will present some data in keeping with this principle.

Notice that, different from other theories, our theory does not define ACWs in negative, by specifying what they are not, but it defines them in positive, clarifying what they are and in what they differ from concrete concepts and words: They do not differ in embodiment, but they differ in acquisition modality, in brain representation and in variability across languages, and they are also likely to differ in the assessment of quantity (see Chap. 1 for this).

2.2 Some Reasons Why Language is so Important for ACWs

As anticipated, we propose that concrete and abstract concepts and words are grounded in perception, action, emotion systems, as well as in linguistic systems, but to a different extent. The difference in grounding between concrete and abstract concepts is a matter of degree: The first are grounded primarily in the sensorimotor system, while ACWs are primarily grounded in the linguistic system. We detail below three main reasons why we think that language plays a major role for ACWs trying to scrutinize the different functions language might play.

Language as glue One of the reasons why language plays a major role in ACWs' representation is given by the heterogeneity and variety of experiences to which typically ACWs refer to. Given the great variety and diversity of the members of abstract categories, using the same word to refer to them can contribute to the category formation. In this sense, as anticipated in Chap. 1, language can work as a sort of glue. A comparison between basic-level concrete concepts and abstract concepts can help to clarify this point.

Consider basic-level concrete concepts, such as "flower" and "hammer". Beyond the diversity of the members of these two categories, we can form a summary mental image of flowers and of hammers (Rosch et al. 1976). In addition, even if all categories continuously change and are updated in light of new exemplars of the category we encounter, concrete concepts are more stable than ACWs. Consider now how the acquisition process of a concrete word such as "flower" works. Children typically hear it in presence of different kinds of flowers, and at the beginning, they might start hypothesizing that it refers to the petals, to the stalk, or to the flower's scent. Then, progressively, they have to learn to refer the word "flower" to roses, cowslips, and daisies, i.e., to different flowers, thus abstracting from the idiosyncratic aspects of each exemplar they have encountered, and they have to learn as well to refer the word to the flower as a whole, not to its parts. Once learned, the word will re-evoke the experience of a flower and will help predict possible actions to perform with flowers—people might be able to imagine a flower, its scent and fragrance, and its color and might be able to prepare themselves to pick up nice flowers. Obviously, the concept of flower to which the word refers will be continuously updated, once new flowers experiences are collected, but somehow, it is not difficult to form an image of the flower's referent.

Take now ACWs such as "truth" or "phantasy," and consider how the acquisition of the word "phantasy" might take place. In this case, it will be much more difficult to refer the word to a single object, and even to a single experience/event. The word "phantasy" might be heard in conjunction with really different situations. Each speaker will associate it to different experiences, but this is not the whole story: The word will be characterized not only by interindividual but also by intraindividual variability: What is "phantasy" for us now might be markedly different from what we associate to "phantasy" in a week. This example highlights that ACWs activate variable, different, and idiosyncratic experiences, and their variability both within individuals and across individuals is greater than the variability that characterizes concrete concepts.

There is however an exception to this variability, represented by nominal kinds (Keil 1989), which are often considered abstract concepts. Nominal kinds are definitional concepts, such as those defined using kinship terms. These concepts might indeed be more anchored to a dictionary definition than other concepts. For example, we all agree, since it has been established within our culture, that aunts are the sisters of one of our parents, or that physicians possess a degree in medicine. Obviously, instability characterizes these concepts as well, but to an extent which is comparable with that of concrete concepts. Concepts of this sort differ indeed from other abstract concepts also because the referent of the corresponding words is typically perceivable through the senses—for example, following the conventions of our culture, we typically represent physicians as wearing a white coat and white shoes.

Overall, the examples we presented show that the meaning of abstract words is usually highly variable, with the exception of the meaning of nominal kinds. Language allows us to cope with this variability and facilitates the acquisition of abstract concepts. With concrete concepts, the environment provides a structure helping kids to learn words (Malt et al. 2010). With abstract words, it is language, conveyed by others, which provides a scaffolding structure helping children understand the meaning. This is the first reason why the presence of a unifying label is particularly precious for ACWs: Possessing a unifying label for diverse and sparse experiences can provide a sort of glue helping keep them together, i.e., it can help to form the category.

Language as social tool An additional reason why language plays a major role for ACWs is due to the social dimension language incorporates. This social dimension might be more relevant for abstract concepts and words since, in order to learn them, we need the contribution of others and of language; this is partially true for all concepts and words, but in different proportions. Consider two verbs such as "to think" and "to pass"; the meaning of the verb "to pass" can be inferred by observing a scene, while the meaning of the verb "to think" cannot. To understand it, the help of others directing our attention, explaining us what is going on, becomes critical. This example clarifies that the social dimension we refer to is not due to the content of the words. For example, in the sentence "Pass me the salt," the concrete verb "to pass" evokes the presence of another person, while in the sentence "I think to go," the abstract verb "to think" does not. Still, according to WAT, the presence of others, their help, and their clarifications would be more crucial to learn the abstract verb "to think" than the concrete verb "to pass."

Importantly, acquiring new abstract words implies a sophisticate social cognition ability: For example, we might need to select the people who have the authority to teach us the meaning of a new word—such as parents in most cases, or experts in a given domain for words we acquire later (Prinz 2002, 2012), or even technological supports as Internet or books for words we acquire late.

The fact that learning of abstract words might occur through the mediation of technological supports is not in contrast with the idea that their acquisition is social, for some reasons. The first is that these linguistically mediated supports are a social and collective product. This might seem not sufficient, since all kinds of artifacts, even cups or bottles, can be considered as social products. The second relies on the theory of simulation: When we read language, we should reactivate the experiences we first had during word acquisition. Relying on a written authoritative source can evoke a situation similar to that in which a real person is explaining to us the word meaning—or using it appropriately (according to Wittgenstein, word meaning has no other explanation than their use). In fact, Borghi et al. 2011) found an effect of written meaning explanations on the representation of ACWs. In the study, which will be described in detail in Chap. 4, page 84–86 (see also Fig. 4.1), participants were presented with novel exemplars of concrete and abstract categories, which were learned observing visual objects; first, they were invited to form categories on a sensorimotor basis, then they were presented with novel labels, and in one condition, they were provided with written explanations of the category meaning. Results of a subsequent property verification task showed that, different from concrete words, abstract words were responded to faster with the mouth, using a microphone, than with the hand, pressing a key on a keyboard; the advantage of the mouth responses with abstract words was particularly marked when explanations were provided. Thus, the written explanations had an influence on representation of the meaning of abstract words. This suggests that, in principle, the idea that the acquisition of ACWs is a social process would hold also in the cases in which a person is alone in a cell and is learning new words from a written text (thanks to people at the ELSP conference for a feedback on that).

Language as material thing As we have seen, abstract concepts refer to entities that are not perceived directly with the senses. But the words to design them, i.e., abstract words, can be obviously perceived with the senses: They are perceived through vision if they are read, through audition if they are listened to, and through both audition and touch/proprioception if they are produced. Importantly, the way in which they are perceived involves actions: Words are produced (spoken, written, etc.) and actively received (listened to, read, etc.). Since concrete words have perceivable referents while abstract words do not, the sensorial dimension provided by the materiality of words (as they are read, written, listened to, or produced) has a higher probability to influence ACWs' representation than the representation of concrete concepts and words.

2.3 What is Crucial in Language? Sounds, Labels, Explanations?

We have seen some of the reasons why, according to WAT, language plays an important role, particularly for ACWs' representation. However, it is important to specify which aspects of language play a role: The phonological properties of words, i.e., their sound? The auditory properties associated to the referents of words, as for example, the sound “mou” associated to cows? The linguistic labels, i.e., the names or verbs or adjectives associated with the concepts? The explanations of the word meaning? We will consider all these four aspects.

2.3.1 Phonology

Let us start with phonology. Are abstract concepts associated with peculiar phonological characteristics, and if it is the case, to what extent does this exert an influence on their representation?

The majority of the studies concern concepts differing in abstraction level, rather than concepts differing in abstractness. Research on categorization has shown that basic-level concepts are characterized by shorter names compared to superordinate ones (e.g., Rosch et al. 1976). Anthropologists have shown that generic species categories are typically named using a single label (e.g., “squirrel,” “cat,” “pine”), while levels subordinate to the basic one are typically named with compound names (e.g., “gray squirrel,” “Persian cat”; “maritime pine”; Berlin et al. 1973). Consistently, both adults and children tend to interpret compounds as referring to subordinate terms. Crucially, this phenomenon holds across languages. (Notice however that the majority of studies pertain English samples; thus, the results might be at least in part biased). Basic-level terms, which are referred to with short names, more typically refer to concrete items, while the hierarchical level is more difficult to determine for abstract terms. For example, “freedom” can be hardly categorized as a basic- or a superordinate-level term.

Recent experimental work shows that the phonological differences do not pertain solely to concepts differing in abstraction level but also to concepts differing in abstractness. In a recent study, Reilly et al. (2012) asked participants to make semantic judgments for nonwords and found that they were more likely to associate an increase in word length and a decrease in word likeness with abstract concepts. Asking participants to decide whether real words were abstract or concrete, they found that they tended to wrongly categorize longer, inflected words (e.g., “apartment”) as abstract and shorter, uninflected abstract words (e.g., “fate”) as concrete. Overall, these results suggest that we are sensitive to statistical regularities in the forms of words and that we distinguish concrete and abstract words also on this basis.

Despite its interest, the phenomenon is not at the focus of our problem that consists in the identification of the aspects of language which are crucial for ACWs’ representation. This result is indeed not necessarily informative on how we represent the meaning of single words, but it mainly concerns the metalinguistic knowledge we possess of classes of words. It tells us on which aspects we rely in representing ACWs as a class, clarifying which elements we take into account when for example we have to evaluate whether a word is abstract or not. Still, interestingly for us, this finding shows that it is very likely that ACWs’ representations are characterized to some extent also by some knowledge on word form, since phonological aspects and meaning are not arbitrarily related.

2.3.2 Auditory Properties

Results of recent work by Lupyan and Thompson-Schill (2012), who investigated how visual categorization is influenced by verbal labels, help us identify the linguistic components which likely influence conceptual representation. In their experiments, participants heard a cue, then they saw a picture and had to respond whether it matched or not with the cue. The cue could for example be a word (e.g., "dog") or a characteristic sound (e.g., a barking sound). The authors demonstrate that verbal labels (e.g., "dog") are more effective than sounds (e.g., the sound of a barking dog) in facilitating visual identification. Labels, reason the authors, have an advantage over sounds for a variety of reasons: because they are words, because they refer to categories, and because they have easily reproducible phonological forms. They demonstrate that nouns are more effective than verbs; hence, the advantage is not due to the fact that verbal labels are words. In addition, nouns are more effective than nonword sound imitation, such as "arf arf" for dog; thus, the advantage of labels is not due exclusively to their sound. (Notice however that the way in which animal calls are encoded in specific languages varies depending on the phonology of languages; thus, a clear distinction should be made between animal sounds and speech sounds.) To note that this result might seem counter-intuitive, since young children call cows "muh muh" and dogs "arf arf" before naming them "cows" and "dogs". Finally, the advantage persists even when novel categories are taught, to which novel labels or sounds are associated. These results indicate that words are not only pointers that index referents (e.g., Glenberg and Robertson 2000), and cast doubts on a view which takes into account only the referential aspect of words. Studies on gestures confirm the fact that reference to a concrete object out in the world is not the default way to make meaning (Mittelberg, personal communication, 2013; Cienki and Mittelberg 2013). In order for a proposition to work and make claims about something, it needs both content and function words (icons and indices, following the terminology of Peirce 1931–1935).

Consider now abstract words. We argued that their representation keeps track of language more than the representation of concrete words. It remains to be determined which aspects of language are more crucial for abstract than for concrete concepts.

In principle, abstract concepts can be grounded in the auditory modality, similar to concrete concepts. Recent results reveal that abstract concepts such as socialism and conservatorism are grounded in different modalities, including the auditory one (Farias et al. 2013). Participants were more likely to evaluate words associated with conservatorism as louder when presented to the right ear than words associated to socialism, even if the sounds did not differ in intensity. This auditory pattern mapped the spatial mapping of the terms, with the words related to conservatorism more oriented to the right and those associated with socialism to the left: The semantic dimension overlaps with the visual and the auditory dimensions. Even if this result concerns a specific subset of abstract concepts, it reveals that abstract concepts can be grounded in the auditory modality, provided that there is an association between sound direction and word meaning. In the same vein, in a study with acronyms of Dutch political parties, van Elk et al. (2010) demonstrated that participants performed button-press responses earlier when the button location corresponded to the political orientation of the party (e.g., they provided faster left responses to left-oriented parties and viceversa); furthermore, responses were faster when a political acronym was displayed on the side of the screen corresponding to the political orientation of its party. The results of these two studies support our view that abstract concepts are both grounded in multimodal dimensions and deeply interwoven in language: As Farias et al. (2013) argue, "an opposition between symbolic representational and modality specific representations is misleading at best" (p. 5).

Even if abstract concepts can be grounded in the auditory modality, the possibility that a sound, as a mooing sound for cows, is more crucial for abstract than for concrete concepts is quite remote, since abstract concepts typically do not have a single, concrete referent, and are therefore difficult to associate to a specific sound. The remoteness of this possibility is empirically confirmed by the negative correlation found by Connell and Lynott (2012) between auditory properties and abstract concepts.

This negative correlation does not contradict our proposal. The perceptual dimension ratings obtained by L&C concern indeed the conceptual referent and the word meaning, not the word per se; for example, the auditory modality would be negatively correlated to the meaning of the abstract word "truth," and not to the meaning of concrete words such as "dog" or "telephone." According to our proposal, the acoustic modality is relevant for abstract concepts because their label and eventually the verbal explanation of their meaning would come to our mind—not the sounds produced by the conceptual referent.

In support of this view, we can briefly refer to the study by Borghi et al. (2011) we introduced on page 24 and that we will extensively illustrate on page 84–86 (see also Figs. 4.1, 4.2, 4.3). In this work, novel categories were used, which were learned observing visual objects, and no sound was associated with them. Even if no sound was associated with the category, nevertheless, results with abstract concepts showed faster and more accurate responses when responding with the microphone, i.e., producing a sound, than when pressing a key on a keyboard; this advantage was not present with concrete concepts. The advantage was more marked when participants were taught not only the label but the explanation of the word meaning as well. This result testifies that the association between the acoustic properties and abstract concepts pertains specifically their labels and the explanations of the word meaning, not the sound elicited by the referent of the category.

In sum, in principle, abstract concepts and words can evoke auditory properties. However, typically, their referents are not associated with specific auditory properties, for the simple reason that it is easier to think of the sound of a telephone than of the sound of the truth. We propose that the linguistic aspects which count more for ACWs' representation are not the sounds/auditory properties of their referents, but their labels.

2.3.3 Labels

The data we have presented lead us to argue that neither the phonological specificity of abstract terms nor the sound of the entities they refer to are at the core of the linguistic representation of ACWs, even if both factors might play a role. In contrast, even if these hypotheses should be tested with further experiments, we predict that two aspects of language might be really relevant for ACWs' representation: labels and explanations.

Labels are relevant for representation of all kinds of concepts and words, as shown by Lupyan and Thompson-Schill (2012). However, we hypothesize that they are particularly crucial for abstract ones, since they facilitate categorization of elements that otherwise would be difficult to classify together.

Literature on word acquisition in children can be informative as to the importance of labels. Many studies have investigated the role played by labels for categorization, with a special focus on how much a common name renders things similar and promotes inferences on their properties. According to one influential view, labels work from the very beginning as category markers, as children expect labels to designate categories and mark their distinctions (e.g., Waxman and Markov 1995). In a well-known study, Gelman and Markman (1986) demonstrated that children use labels as indicators of a category, then they generalize properties to that category. In their study, the authors had triads of elements. They taught children hidden properties of one of the elements of the triad (e.g., "it has hollow bones") and found that children tended to generalize the property to the element of the triad that had the same name but was perceptually dissimilar rather than to the perceptually similar element which had a different name. These results, however, were challenged by Sloutsky and Fisher (2004) who demonstrated with the same stimuli used by Gelman and Markman (1986) that children's behavior cannot be predicted relying only on labels, but that only a model based on both labels and appearance can accurately predict their performance. Sloutsky and collaborators have also argued that labels contribute in increasing category similarity and have shown that early in development, labels work like other perceptual features such as shape, color, and size. Only later, in the course of development, they start to be perceived as category markers. For example, Deng and Sloutsky (2012) investigated the role played by labels for categorization in children aged four and five as well as in adults. They found that adults use labels against perceptual similarity, while this is not the case for children. In addition, they found that early in development, labels work as other features, such as shape and size, but later during the development, in adulthood, they become crucial to indicate the category, marking the distinctions between different categories.

Now, consider abstract concepts. It is possible that during the acquisition of ACWs, labels work also as category markers. Since running on the grass, exiting prison, and taking a decision without the influence of others do not have much in common, but can all be categorized as experiences of "freedom," using the same label to designate them will be really helpful for building the category. The presence of the same name can indeed direct attention in a top-down manner (Gliga et al. 2010), guiding learning, thus helping people to collect the sparse and diverse experiences that can be associated with a specific category. To our knowledge, the debate on labels as category markers has focused on concrete words and has not dealt with the differences between kinds of words. This is probably due to the fact that children acquire ACWs later than concrete concepts and words.

We propose that the top-down mechanism according to which labels guide learning characterizes the acquisition of ACWs, for two reasons. The first is that their members can be really diverse from a perceptual and motor point of view; the second is that ACWs are acquired relatively late in the course of development, as data on age of acquisition reveal (Della Rosa et al. 2010). We are not fully in keeping with the labels-as-category markers approach, though. In particular, we do not think it is very useful when it contrasts labels and perceptual similarity (see Deng and Sloutsky 2012, for a similar view), since typically the same label is correlated with a higher perceptual similarity between the category members. Even if referents of ACWs are not perceptually similar, they might have common characteristics derived from similar experiences, or they might rely on common image schemas (Barsalou 1999). For example, all experiences of freedom might include a reference to the self, and crossing of a boundary or absence of a boundary. As anticipated in the first part of the chapter, ACWs are grounded in multimodal experiences, and among these experiences, the linguistic one has a special status.

In support of this view, Borghi et al. (2011) and Granito et al. (in preparation) found with novel objects that the use of labels helps more the formation of abstract than of concrete categories. More specifically, Borghi et al. (2011) found that the disadvantage in processing of abstract over concrete concepts is maintained, but slightly reduced when people are taught labels to apply to categories.

Notice that Borghi et al. used written labels in their word acquisition study with adults, but acoustically presented labels are probably the most effective with children. In infancy (6–10 months), the acoustic modality dominates indeed over the visual one (for a review, see Lewkowicz 1994). Sloutsky and Napolitano (2003) demonstrated that not only infants but children as well (4 year olds) have a preference for acoustic over visual modalities: When submitted with combinations of visual and acoustic stimuli (scenes associated with a sound), they made equivalence judgments on the basis of the auditory components rather than of the visual one, and they encoded more readily the acoustic than the visual components.

2.3.4 Explanations

Borghi et al. (2011) found that not only labels but also explanations of the word meaning play a role and influence object processing and that explanations are more effective to learn abstract word meanings than concrete ones. That of explanation is a function of language not considered by Lupyan and Thomson-Schill. There are cases in which the meaning of a category has to be learned, thanks to the contribution of other members of our community. As argued by Prinz (2002), to learn the word "democracy," we may visualize a series of scenes, but also rely on the opinion of authoritative members of our community. Other people can help us understand abstract concepts providing us with explanations, or furnishing us a list of possible instances of the category. When hearing or reading new terms, we often search for their meaning on the dictionary, or look up their meaning on Wikipedia. The role played by explanation can be seen as in contrast with the idea advanced by Wittgenstein of language games, since it anchors concepts to a specific meaning, and with the idea that what counts is not the explanation of word meaning but their use. We believe it is not. Providing explanations consists indeed in providing a context where the word can be found, as well as in highlighting the relationship between the elements that the word evokes.

Consider that the explanations to account for abstract terms meaning are typically longer than those that can be used to explain concrete word meaning, since in the last case, the external environment can provide much more scaffolding and support. For example, explaining the meaning of "democracy" requires many more words than explaining the meaning of "bottle," also due to the fact that in the last case a bottle can be shown to the learner (see Chap. 4 for further details on studies on modality of acquisition (MOA); e.g., Wauters et al. 2003).

Underlying the role of explanations, we stress a peculiarity of language, which is often neglected. Nobody would obviously deny that language has social nature. However, theorists belonging to the different approaches have not pointed out the sociality of language in the way we do in our proposal.

Theorists favoring a pragmatic view have focused mostly on the communicative aspects of language: Their claim that language can be conceived (of) as a form of action which changes and modifies the surrounding world is important for us. More recently, theorists favoring an embodied and grounded cognition perspective have emphasized mostly the fact that language is grounded in perception and action systems. According to a third recent approach, word meanings would be determined by the statistical distribution of words across language (e.g., Landauer and Dumais 1997; Griffiths et al. 2007). Recent proposals have shown that the last two approaches are not necessarily conflicting but can be reconciled (e.g., Andrews et al. 2013; Louwerse 2011; Meteyard et al. 2012; Borghi and Caruana in press). We are completely sympathetic with the view that embodied/grounded and distributional approaches can be reconciled (see for example Borghi and Cimatti 2012). However, here we intend to claim something more. In our view, language can work as a communicative/action device (pragmatic), as a pointer (embodied and grounded view), and its meaning can be determined by a network of associated words (distributional view). The social dimension of language enters into play in all these approaches. However, we think that the way we represent language—and abstract words in particular—does not only keep track of the frequency of occurrence of associated words, but also of the relevance/authority (for us) of the members (e.g., parents, authoritative members of our community) who explained to us the meaning of words. These "sociological" aspects would have a mental counterpart and cognitive consequences. In this sense, we believe that the social aspects intrinsic in language can influence the way concepts and words are acquired and therefore represented.

Summarizing, in Sect. 2.3, we have scrutinized different aspects of language that can be relevant for ACWs' representation. We propose that, even if phonological and auditory properties might play some role, they are not as crucial as verbal labels and explanations in influencing ACWs' representation.

2.4 Which Mechanisms?

So far, we have clarified the role that different linguistic aspects—phonology, acoustic properties, labels, and explanations—might have in influencing the representation of ACWs. Direct evidence in favor of the WAT view will be presented more extensively in the next chapters. Here, we outline a proposal concerning the different mechanisms that might underlie the activation of linguistic information for ACWs. This proposal is currently speculative and needs to be verified with appropriate experimental evidence.

Let us start with some recent evidence which needs to be accounted for. In a recent study, Ghio et al. (2013) analyzed three different kinds of abstract sentences—sentences referring to emotions, to mental states, and to math concepts—and compared them to concrete sentences describing actions with three different effectors: hand, legs, and mouth. Participants had to rate all sentences on concreteness, context availability, familiarity, and body part involvement using 7-point scales. The authors found that, when required, participants associated abstract sentences with effectors. Specifically, mental states and emotional sentences were more associated with the mouth effector than with the legs and hands, while math concepts evoked preferentially the hands. This activation of the mouth with most typical abstract concepts is predicted by the WAT. In our view, this is likely due to the acquisition process of abstract concepts, which occurs mainly through the mediation of language, as discussed in the course of the book. The results by Borghi et al. (2011), by Scorolli et al. (2012), and by Granito et al. (in preparation) go in the same direction. The evidence by Ghio et al. concerns participants' associations; hence, it is metalinguistic; the evidence by Scorolli et al. (2012) is obtained with a TMS study, while the evidence by Borghi et al. and Granito et al. pertains to production of a motor response with the mouth.

To account for evidence as the described one, we would need to understand more in depth what happens and what phenomena are at the basis of the mouth activation with ACWs. We will outline below some possible mechanisms that might underlie the effects found. These mechanisms are not mutually exclusive—most probably they are all present. Two pertain more the memory traces we keep of the way in which we acquired the concepts, two the ways in which these concepts are processed online.

It is possible that the motor activation of the mouth effector depends on traces of acoustic experiences evoked while listening to or while producing the verbal labels and the explanations of word meaning. Alternatively, the mouth activation can be due to a form of motor preparation, aimed at the rehearsal of the label or of the explanation associated with the word meaning. Finally, it can be due to some kind of inner language.

The notion of inner language requires some further clarification. As highlighted by Vygotsky (1978, 1986) and also by supporters of the extended mind view, as the philosopher Andy Clark (Clark and Chalmers 1998; Clark 2008), language is initially a social and public phenomenon, which becomes internalized during the course of development. This internalization allows children and later adults to use a form of inner speech, which guides their actions and has the power to augment their computational abilities and abstract thought capabilities (see also Clark 1998). Consider for example the cases in which we use language to remember some dancing steps, or when verbalizations helps us compute or solve some difficult problem. We propose that not only external, public language, but inner speech as well might play a role for ACWs. Abstract, difficult notions do indeed require more internal elaboration, hence more inner speech, as if we need to retell and re-explain to ourselves their meaning. The advantage of this interpretation is that it helps reconcile the WAT account of abstract concepts with the idea, proposed by Barsalou and Wiemer Hastings (2005) and discussed in Chap. 3, that introspection plays a major role for abstract concepts and the data showing that introspective properties are more frequent with abstract than with concrete concepts. It extends Barsalou and Wiemer Hastings's (2005) view clarifying how introspection might occur, i.e., through the mediation of a form of inner speech which involves the mouth.

Since production and comprehension systems are two faces of the same coin (Pickering and Garrod 2013) and rely on the same neural substrates, as shown for example by recent literature on mirror neuron activation (e.g., D'Ausilio et al. 2009), the different mechanisms can be hard to disentangle. In fact, literature on the mirror neuron system has shown that part of the neural circuitry involved in the execution of motor actions is also activated during the comprehension of language referring to those actions. (Gallese et al. 1996; Jirak et al. 2010; review in Rizzolatti and Craighero 2004, and many others).

A, B, C, and D are all compatible with the evidence of Borghi et al. (2011) of an activation of the mouth effector, particularly when an explanation of its meaning was provided, with TMS data by Scorolli et al. (2012) which suggest an activation of the mouth effector with noun–verb combinations where an abstract verb is present and with fMRI results by Sakreida et al. (2013) which show an activation of the linguistic neural network with combinations composed by an abstract verb and an abstract noun (see Chap. 5 for further discussion of this evidence). One could object that the results found by Borghi et al. did not concern acoustically presented explanations, but written ones. However, a written text typically re-evokes the experience of its acoustic presentation. Furthermore, evidence by Granito et al. (in preparation) concerns more directly verbally produced explanations and is compatible with A–D accounts (see Chap. 4 for a detailed description of these experiments). Finally, the four mechanisms are compatible with the association Ghio et al. (2013) found between the mouth effectors and ACWs.

All mechanisms we have proposed so far share one problem. It is not clear why the association between ACWs and the mouth effector does not hold for number concepts, which according to Ghio et al. (2013) are considered as more associated with the hand than with the mouth effector. One possible explanation is that number concepts are a very special kind of abstract concepts, since the experience of finger counting (Fischer and Brugger 2011; Fischer 2008, 2011; Lindemann et al. 2011; Badets and Pesenti 2010; Ranzini et al. 2011) (see Fig. 2.2) provides a clear way to scaffold them.

A further problem that might lead to favor the first two memory-based mechanisms is the evidence by Borghi et al. (2011) who showed a stronger motor activation of the mouth when written explanations were provided. However, the fact that explanations have a motor effect, activating the mouth, is not necessarily in conflict with the activation of internal language—it is indeed possible that we retell ourselves the meaning of the concept, as it occurs in silent reading, when people pronounce each word they read.

Overall, the four possible mechanisms we propose are the following:

a. memory traces of listened labels and explanations;
b. memory traces of the experience of producing the label and the explanation;
c. motor preparation, aimed at rehearsal of the label or of the explanation;
d. motor activation due to inner language.

While current experimental evidence indicates that the mouth is more activated with ACWs, it does not allow to disentangle among them. It is also possible that more mechanisms are activated at the same time. Further experimental evidence is necessary to investigate and to better understand the processes that take place and the specific mechanisms responsible for the activation of the mouth with ACWs.

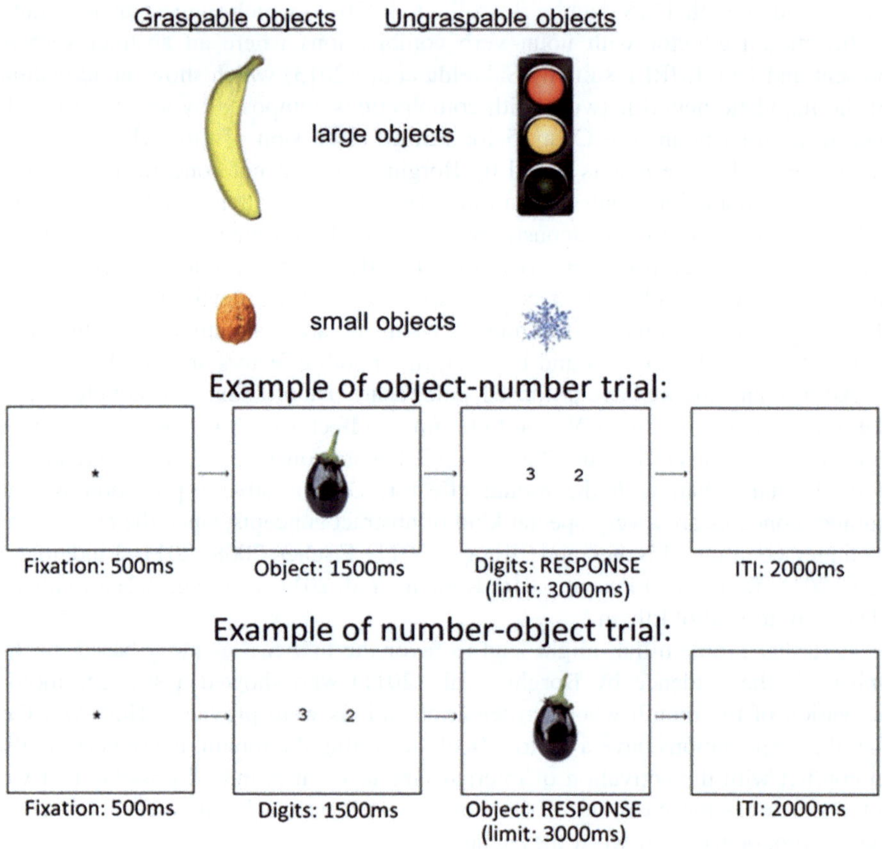

Fig. 2.2 Study by Ranzini et al. (2011). Participants were presented with digits and with images of graspable and non-graspable objects of different size (large vs. small). Their task consisted in repeating aloud the odd or even digit within a pair depending on the object type. The digits could precede or follow the object presentation. Responses were faster for graspable than non-graspable objects preceded by numbers; results revealed also an effect of numerical magnitude after the presentation of graspable objects. Overall results suggest that graspable objects facilitate number processing, supporting the view that abstract concepts as numbers are grounded in sensorimotor experience

2.5 Conclusion: WAT and the Scaffolding Role of Language

In this chapter, we have sketched a proposal concerning the representation of ACWs, the WAT proposal. The most crucial distinguishing aspect of this proposal is that it holds that the acquisition of ACWs relies more on language and on the contribution of other people to the clarification of word meaning. Due to the fact that the scaffolding function of the physical environment is less powerful for abstract than for concrete concepts, language helps filling this gap. This dominance of language is reflected in the way we represent ACWs in the brain, and it has a motor counterpart, i.e., it implies the activation of the mouth effector. We outlined some mechanisms that might underlie the activation of the mouth effector. Further research is needed to further detail them and to get a better understanding of what is going on when we use an abstract concept. In addition, further research is needed in order to understand whether this proposal can hold for all abstract concepts or only for a subset of them. To this aim, a fine-grained analysis of the different kinds of abstract concepts is badly needed.

In the next chapter, we will distinguish the WAT view from other proposals in the field. In the further chapters, we will critically discuss the evidence obtained so far which favors the WAT view and we will illustrate what kind of further evidence is needed to fully support it.

References

Andrews, M., Frank, S. & Vigliocco, G. (2013). Reconciling embodied and distributional accounts of meaning in language. *Topics in Cognitive Science.*

Badets, A., & Pesenti, M. (2010). Creating number semantics through finger movement perception. *Cognition, 115*, 46–53.

Barsalou, L. W. (1999). Perceptual symbol systems. *Behavioral and Brain Sciences, 22*, 577–609.

Barsalou, L. W., & Wiemer-Hastings, K. (2005). Situating abstract concepts. In D. Pecher & R. Zwaan (Eds.), *Grounding cognition: The role of perception and action in memory, language, and thought* (pp. 129–163). New York: Cambridge University Press.

Berlin, B., Breedlove, D., & Raven, P. (1973). General principles of classification and nomenclature in folk biology. *American Anthropologist, 74*, 214–242.

Borghi, A.M., & Caruana, F. (in press). Embodiment theories. In J. Wright (Ed.) *International encyclopedia of the social and behavioral sciences* (2nd ed.). S. Cappa (Ed.) Section of cognitive neuroscience.

Borghi, A. M., & Cimatti, F. (2009). Words as tools and the problem of abstract words meanings. In N. Taatgen & H. van Rijn (Eds.), *Proceedings of the 31st Annual Conference of the Cognitive Science Society* (pp. 2304–2309). Amsterdam: Cognitive Science Society.

Borghi, A.M., & Cimatti, F. (2012). Words are not just words: the social acquisition of abstract words. *RIFL*—ISSN: 2036-6728, doi:10.4396/20120303

Borghi, A. M., Flumini, A., Cimatti, F., Marocco, D., & Scorolli, C. (2011). Manipulating objects and telling words: A study on concrete and abstract words acquisition. *Frontiers in Psychology, 2*, 15. doi:10.3389/fpsyg.2011.00015

Cangelosi, A., & Parisi, D. (1998). The emergence of a "language" in an evolving population of neural networks. *Connection Science, 10*, 83–97.

Cienki, A., & Mittelberg, I. (2013). Creativity in the forms and functions of gestures with speech. In T. Veale, K. Feyaerts, & C. Forceville (Eds.), *Creativity and the agile mind: A multi-disciplinary study of a multi-faceted phenomenon (applications of cognitive linguistics)* (pp. 231–252). Berlin/New York: Mouton de Gruyter.

Clark, A. (2008). *Supersizing the mind. Embodiment action, and cognitive extension.* Oxford: Oxford University Press.

Clark, A., & Chalmers, D. (1998). The extended mind. *Analysis, 58*, 7–19.

Connell, L., & Lynott, D. (2012). Strength of perceptual experience predicts word processing performance better than concreteness or imageability. *Cognition, 125*(3), 452–465.

D'Ausilio, A., Pulvermueller, F., Salmas, P., Bufalari, I., Begliomini, C., & Fadiga, L. (2009). The motor somatotopy of speech perception. *Current Biology, 19*(5), 381–385.

Deng, W., & Sloutsky, V.M. (2012). The role of linguistic labels in inductive generalization. *Journal of Experimental Child Psychology*, http://dx.doi.org/10.1016/j.jecp.2012.10.011

Della Rosa, P.A., Catricalà, E., Vigliocco, G., & Cappa, S.F. (2010). Beyond the abstract-concrete dichotomy: mode of acquisition, concreteness, imageability, familiarity, age of acquisition, context availability, and abstractness norms for a set of 417 Italian words. *Behavioral Research Methods*, *42*(4), 1042–1048

Farias, A. R., Garrido, M. V., & Semin, G. R. (2013). Converging modalities ground abstract categories: The case of politics. *PLoS ONE, 8*(4), e60971. doi:10.1371/journal.pone.0060971

Fischer, M. H. (2008). Finger counting habits modulate spatial-numerical associations. *Cortex, 44*, 386–392.

Fischer, M. H. (2011). The spatial mapping of numbers—its origin and flexibility. In Y. Coello & A. Bartolo (Eds.), *Language and action in cognitive neurosciences*. London: Psychology Press.

Fischer, M. H., & Brugger, P. (2011). When digits help digits: spatial–numerical associations point to finger counting as prime example of embodied cognition. *Frontiers in Psychology, 2*, 260. doi:10.3389/fpsyg.2011.00260

Gallese, V., Fogassi, L., Fadiga, L., & Rizzolatti, G. (1996). Action recognition in the premotor cortex. *Brain, 119*, 593–609.

Gelman, S. A., & Markman, E. (1986). Categories and induction in young children. *Cognition, 23*, 183–209.

Ghio, M., Vaghi, M.M.S., & Tettamanti, M. (2013). Fine-grained semantic categorization across the abstract and concrete omains. *PLoS ONE, 8*(6): e67090. doi:10.1371/journal.pone.0067090

Glenberg, A. M., & Robertson, D. A. (2000). Symbol grounding and meaning: A comparison of high-dimensional and embodied theories of meaning. *Journal of Memory and Language, 43*, 379–401.

Granito, C., Scorolli, C., & Borghi, A.M. (in preparation). Alice in Legoland: A study on abstract words acquisition.

Gliga, T., Volein, A., & Csibra, G. (2010). Verbal labels modulate perceptual object processing in one-year-old infants. *Journal of Cognitive Neuroscience, 22*, 2781–2789.

Griffiths, T. L., Steyvers, M., & Tenenbaum, J. B. (2007). Topics in semantic representation. *Psychological Review, 114*(2), 211–244.

Jirak, D., Menz, M., Buccino, G., Borghi, A. M., & Binkofski, F. (2010). Grasping language. A short story on embodiment. *Consciousness and Cognition, 19*, 711–720.

Keil, F. C. (1989). *Concepts, kinds and cognitive development*. London: MIT Press.

Landauer, T., & Dumais, S. (1997). A solutions to Plato's problem: the latent semantic analysis theory of acquisition, induction and representation of knowledge. *Psychological Review, 104*, 211–240.

Lewkowicz, D. J. (1994). The development of intersensory perception in human infants. In D. J. Lewkowicz & R. Lickliter (Eds.), *The development of perception: Comparative perspectives* (pp. 165–203). Hillsdale: Erlbaum.

Lindemann, O., Alipour, A., & Fischer, M. H. (2011). Finger counting habits in Middle-Eastern and Western individuals: An online survey. *Journal of Cross-Cultural Psychology, 42*, 566–578.

Louwerse, M. M. (2011). Symbol interdependency in symbolic and embodied cognition. *Topics in Cognitive Science, 3*, 273–302.

Lugli, L., Baroni, G., Gianelli, C., Borghi, A.M., Nicoletti, R. (2012). Self, others, objects: How this triadic interaction modulates our behavior. *Memory and Cognition*, *40*, 1373–1386

Lupyan, G. (2012). What do words do? Toward a theory of language-augmented thought. In B. H. Ross (Ed.), *The psychology of learning and motivation* (Vol. 57, pp. 255–297). London: Academic Press.

Lupyan, G., & Thompson-Schill, S. L. (2012). The evocative power of words: Activation of concepts by verbal and nonverbal means. *Journal of Experimental Psychology: General, 141*(1), 170–186.

Malt, B., Gennari, S., & Imai, M. (2010). Lexicalization patterns and the world to words mapping. In B. C. Malt & S. Wolff (Eds.), *Words and the mind. How words capture new experience*. New York: Oxford University Press.

Meteyard, L., Cuadrado, S. R., Bahrami, B., & Vigliocco, G. (2012). Coming of age: A review of embodiment and the neuroscience of semantics. *Cortex, 48*, 788–804.

Mittelberg, I. (2013). The exbodied mind: Cognitive-semiotic principles as motivating forces in gesture. In: C. Müller, A. Cienki, E. Fricke, S.H. Ladewig, D. McNeill & S. Tessendorf (eds.), *Body—language—communication: An international handbook on multimodality in human interaction. Handbooks of linguistics and communication science* (Vol. 38(1), pp. 750–779). Berlin: Mouton de Gruyter.

Peirce, C. S. (1931–1935, 1958). In: C. Hartshorne & P. Weiss (Eds.) *Collected papers of Charles Sanders Peirce*, vols. 1–6 (1931–35), A. W. Burks (Ed.), vols. 7–8 (1958), Cambridge: Harvard University Press.

Pickering, M. J., & Garrod, S. (2013). An integrated theory of language production and comprehension. *Behavioral and Brain Sciences, 36*(4), 329–347.

Prinz, J. J. (2002). *Furnishing the mind concepts and their perceptual basis*. Cambridge: MIT Press.

Prinz, J. J. (2012). *Beyond human nature*. London: Penguin.

Ranzini, M., Lugli, L., Anelli, M., Carbone, R., Nicoletti, R., & Borghi, A.M. (2011). Graspable objects shape number processing. *Frontiers in Human Neuroscience, 5*, art.147, doi:10.3389/fnhum.2011.00147

Reilly, J., Westbury, C., Kean, J., & Peelle, J. E. (2012). Arbitrary symbolism in natural language revisited: When word forms carry meaning. *PLoS ONE, 7*(8), e42286. doi:10.1371/journal.pone.0042286

Rizzolatti, G., & Craighero, L. (2004). The mirror neuron system. *Annual Review of Neuroscience, 27*, 169–192.

Rosch, E., Mervis, C. B., Gray, W. D., Johnson, D. M., & Boyews-Braem, P. (1976). Basic level in natural categories. *Cognitive Psychology, 8*, 382–439.

Sakreida, K., Scorolli, C., Menz, M.M., Heim, S., Borghi, A.M.,& Binkofski, F. (2013). Are abstract action words embodied? An fMRI investigation at the interface between language and motor cognition. *Frontiers in Human Neuroscience, 7*, 125

Scorolli, C., Jacquet, P., Binkofski, F., Nicoletti, R., Tessari, A., & Borghi, A.M. (2012). Abstract and concrete phrases processing differently modulates cortico-spinal excitability. *Brain Research, 1488*, 60–71. doi:10.1016/j.brainres.2012.10.004

Sloutsky V.M., & Fisher, A.V. (2004). When development and learning decrease memory. Evidence against category-based induction in children. *Psychological science, 15*(8), 533–548

Sloutsky V.M., & Napolitano, A.C. (2003). Is a picture worth a thousand words? Preference for auditory modality in children. *Child Development, 74*(3), 822–33

van Elk, M., van Schie, H. T., & Bekkering, H. (2010). From left to right: Processing acronyms referring to names of political parties activates spatial associations. *Quarterly Journal of Experimental Psychology, 63*(11), 2202–2219.

Vygotsky, L.S. (1978). Mind in Society. Cambridge, MA: Harvard University Press

Vygotsky, L.S. (1986). Thought and language. Cambridge, MA: MIT Press.

Wauters, L.N., Tellings, A.E.J.M., van Bon, W.H.J., & van Haaften, A.W. (2003). Mode of acquisition of word meanings: The viability of a theoretical construct. *Applied Psycholinguistics, 24*, 385–406

Waxman, S.R., & Markow, D.B. (1995). Words as invitations to form categories: Evidence from 12–13-month-old infants. *Cognitive Psychology, 29*, 257–302

Yoshida, H. & Smith, L.B. (2005). Linguistic cues enhance the learning of perceptual cues. *Psychological Science, 16*(2), 90–95

Chapter 3
Embodied and Hybrid Theories of Abstract Concepts and Words

To say it another way, thinking, however abstract, originates in an embodied subjectivity, at once overdetermined and permeable to contingent events.

Teresa de Lauretis

3.1 Introduction

So far different theories of abstract concepts and words representation have been proposed. Below, we will illustrate the main approaches to abstract concepts and words, highlighting their strengths and weaknesses and underlying the similarities and differences between the other theories and our proposal. We will start with embodied theories.

We will first outline theories according to which abstract and concrete concepts do not differ as they are both grounded in action, emotion, and force dynamics. Then, we will illustrate theories which, even if maintaining an embodied stance, argue that abstract and concrete concepts are grounded on different aspects, for example situations versus perceptual properties and direct experience versus metaphors.

Finally, we will illustrate recent approaches arguing for the necessity of a double representation, some of which stem from the classical theory of Paivio. We will outline as well recent theories that, even if not referred directly to abstract concepts, are relevant for our understanding of them.

3.2 Grounding in Action of both Concrete and Abstract Concepts

Within embodied and grounded (EG) theories, we can distinguish two main approaches to abstract concepts. According to the classical EG view, abstract concepts are not special: They are EG exactly as concrete concepts. Other EG views recognize that abstract and concrete concepts differ in content, even if both are embodied and grounded.

In this section, we will illustrate the approach according to which abstract and concrete concepts do not differ. Various research lines provide pieces of evidence

A. M. Borghi and F. Binkofski, *Words as Social Tools: An Embodied View on Abstract Concepts*, SpringerBriefs in Cognition,
DOI: 10.1007/978-1-4614-9539-0_3, © The Author(s) 2014

suggesting that the representations of the two kinds of concepts at least partially overlap (for a thorough review, see Pecher et al. 2011). According to the proponents of this view, their representations partially overlap since both concrete and abstract concepts are grounded in action (see ACE and approach–avoidance effect) and in force dynamics.

A first line of research underlines the role of action in abstract concepts representation. This view is based on evidence of the so-called "action–sentence compatibility effect" (ACE for short), obtained with both concrete and abstract transfer sentences, using both behavioral and TMS methods (Glenberg and Kaschak 2002; Glenberg et al. 2008a, b). The ACE consists in faster responses when the action implied by a sentence (e.g., "open" vs. "close a drawer") matches with the action performed to produce a response (pressing a button moving toward vs. away from the body). Glenberg and Kaschak (2002) found an ACE with both concrete (e.g., "Andy delivered the pizza to you/You delivered the pizza to Andy") and abstract transfer sentences (e.g., "Liz told you the story/You told Liz the story"). However, as Glenberg et al. (2008a, b) argue, while for concrete sentences, the simulation evoked can explain the ACE interaction found with manual responses, it is more difficult to account for it with abstract sentences: For example, "You tell Liz the story" would imply the activation of the neural substrate for mouth, not for hand moving. According to Glenberg et al. (2008a, b), we would develop an action schema, which underlies different transfer verbs (handle, give, etc.) even if the specific parameters, such as those related to the kind of grip, might differ. The same schema would be generalized to abstract transfer sentences. In support of this view, the authors used a sentence sensibility evaluation task applying single-pulse transcranial magnetic stimulation to hand muscles. They found a greater motor system modulation (larger MEPS) when participants read both concrete and abstract transfer sentences (e.g., concrete transfer sentences: "Marco gives you the papers. You give the papers to Marco"; abstract transfer sentences: "Anna delegates the responsibilities to you. You delegate the responsibilities to Anna."), compared to sentences that did not refer to transfer (e.g., "You read the papers with Marco. You discuss the responsibilities with Anna."). The MEPs modulation was similar with concrete and abstract transfer sentences, both when the pulse was delivered at the verb presentation and at the end of the sentence. This confirms that simulation of concrete transfer underlies comprehension of both concrete and abstract sentences. Further studies have found the ACE demonstrating that the abstract quantifiers "more" and "less" activate an upward versus a downward movement (Guan et al. 2013). Similarly, recent evidence in our laboratory has shown that calculation processes such as summing or subtracting are associated to different bodily movements (see Fig. 3.1).

Participants had to make additions or subtractions while performing an ascending and a descending movement, using a lift or taking the stairs. We found a congruency effect between the bodily movement direction and the kind of calculation: Addition was associated to an ascending movement with the lift, subtraction with a descending movement (Lugli et al. 2013). The effect was not present with the stairs, likely due to the fact that the movement associated with the

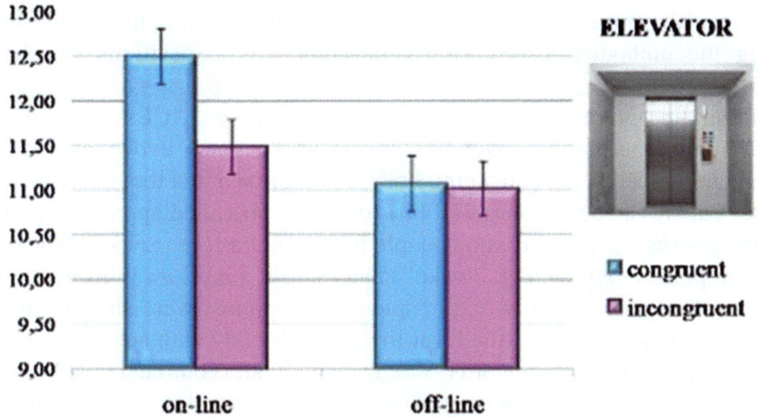

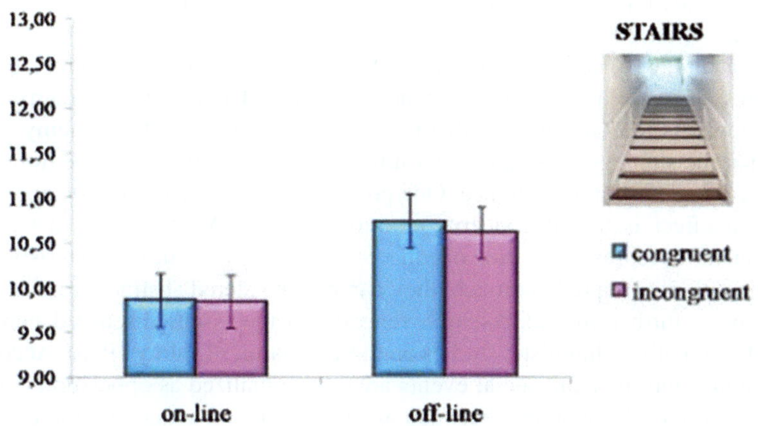

Fig. 3.1 Study by Lugli et al. (2013). The interaction between kind of operation and movement showing an advantage of the congruent condition (addition and ascending movement, subtraction and descending movement) over the incongruent one (addition and descending movement, subtraction and ascending movement) when participants used the elevator but not the stairs. The congruency effect was present only when participants performed the task during the execution of the movement (*online* condition), not when they performed it after having executed it (*offline* condition). The result supports the idea that numbers and calculation processes are grounded in the sensorimotor system

elevator is more clearly vertical and faster. The absence of a congruency effect when the calculations were made after the movement (off-line condition), and when the movement was not directly experienced but simply imagined, indicates the effect is motor and not only perceptual. The result suggests not only that larger quantities are associated with an upward movement, smaller quantities with a downward movement, but also that the different calculation processes are associated with movements differing in direction. Overall, they contribute in revealing the embodied nature of spatial-numerical associations (Fischer and Brugger 2011).

A further line of research, very related to the one on ACEs, has shown that (abstract) emotional terms, such as "love" or "anger," evoke approach and avoidance movements, thus engaging both the emotional and the motor system. In a seminal paper, Chen and Bargh (1999) found the so-called approach–avoidance effect: Responses were faster when people had to pull a lever toward their body in response to positive words (e.g., "cake") and to push a level away from their body in response to negative words (e.g., "spider"); responses were slower when participants were required to pull the lever toward their body with negative words and to push it away with positive words. Van Dantzig et al. (2008) extended this result showing that approach/avoidance movements are encoded in terms of their outcome, not of the specific movement: In contrast to negative words, positive ones evoke the tendency to reduce the distance between the stimulus and the self (see also Freina et al. 2009; Förster and Strack 1996) (see Fig. 3.2).

Lugli et al. (2012) and Gianelli et al. (2013) recently introduced and manipulated the addressee of the action using sentences such as "The object is attractive/ugly. Bring it towards you/Give it to another person/Give it to a friend/to an enemy." They found that the simulated social context influenced the kinematics of the movement and the coding of stimulus valence. One problem of the evidence on the approach–avoidance effect is that it concerns emotional terms: As discussed in Chap. 1, emotional terms represent a subset of concepts with idiosyncratic characteristics, and depending on the adopted approach, they can be considered abstract or not.

Finally, a further line of research relevant to the issues discussed here was inspired by cognitive linguistic studies on force dynamics (Talmy 1988). According to the author, physical and social events are conceptualized as opposition between conflicting forces, for example between an agonist and an antagonist force. This is true also for linguistically described events. In Talmy's view, the representation of both concrete and abstract events relies on the same force mechanisms; the only difference is that in the last case, the agonist tends more toward rest or performs less "physical" actions (see for a thorough review Pecher et al. 2011). In a submitted paper (reported in Pecher et al. 2011), Madden and Pecher (2010) reported evidence favoring this view: When primed by two shapes that interacted according to the same force dynamics pattern, sentence sensibility judgments were faster than in mismatch cases. In support of Talmy's view, this reveals that the availability of force dynamics information facilitates processing; importantly, as predicted by Talmy, results were the same for concrete and abstract sentences. Even though the theory is fascinating and the evidence found is compelling, it might be difficult to extend it to cases in which single concepts instead of whole sentences are considered.

Overall, the three research areas we illustrated have some communality. Researchers from these three areas, supported by rich and compelling evidence, underline the similarities rather than the differences between concrete and abstract concepts, showing that both are grounded in action. The three areas have some common limitations, though: in all cases, the evidence provided is confined to

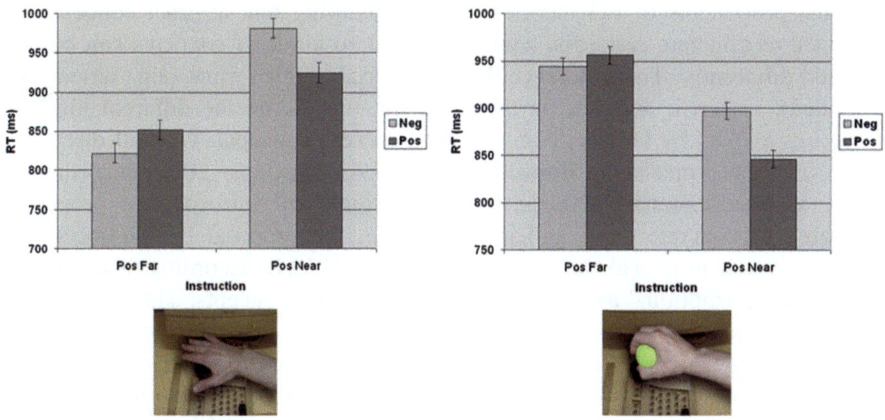

Fig. 3.2 Study by Freina et al. (2009). Participants had to classify a word as positive or negative. They had to respond pressing a near or far key on the keyboard, performing a movement either toward or away from their body. When they responded holding a tennis ball in their hand, they were faster when pressing the near key for positive objects and the far key for negative objects. When they responded with the empty, open hand the results were the opposite: Response times were faster when pressing the "far" button for positive words and the "near" button for negative words, as if they "simulated" reaching for something "good" and avoiding something "bad." Overall, results show that emotion terms are grounded in the sensorimotor system and reveal that there exists a complex interplay between emotional words, movement, and hand posture

specific domains—to transfer sentences for ACE evidence, to the emotional domain for approach–avoidance effects, and to the events that can be conceptualized in terms of force dynamics for work inspired by Talmy's view. It is hard to foresee how far this evidence can be extended to other domains. Furthermore, it remains open the possibility that, although concrete and abstract words do not differ in the dimensions considered, they differ along other dimensions.

In line with the perspective presented in this section, the WAT view proposes that both concrete and abstract concepts are grounded in perception and action, and thus their representations overlap for some important aspects. However, we believe that this is not the whole story and that it would be important to find ways to operationalize the distinctions and not only the commonalities between concrete and abstract concepts.

3.3 Differences in Content Between Concrete and Abstract Concepts

Much of the debate on abstract and concrete concepts focuses on their differences—in format, in grounding, and in the constituent semantic attributes. In this and in the next section, we will discuss proposals and evidence emphasizing the differences rather than the similarities between concrete and abstract concepts.

Some proponents of EG theories, though claiming that abstract concepts are grounded as concrete concepts, admit that the two kinds of concepts can be represented differently. The difference does not pertain their format (e.g., amodal vs. grounded); rather, it depends on their content, that is, on the different kinds of properties evoked by abstract compared to concrete concepts. We will discuss in Sect. 3.3.1 the proposal by Barsalou and Wiemer-Hastings (2005) according to which abstract concepts activate more situations and introspective properties compared to concrete ones, and in Sect. 3.3.2, the proposal by Vigliocco and collaborators (Kousta et al. 2011; Vigliocco et al. 2013a, b) according to which they activate more emotional aspects compared to concrete concepts. The two theories have in common the embodied stance, as well as the fact that they ascribe the difference between concrete and abstract concepts to their differences in content. In addition, different from other proposals, they do not only provide a negative definition of abstract concepts (e.g., concepts less imageable and less sensory-based than concrete ones) (see Vigliocco et al. 2013a, b, for a similar critique against Paivio's view, and Paivio 2013) but they propose that different semantic features characterize the two kinds of concepts: Concrete concepts evoke more perceptual properties, abstract ones more situations and introspective properties (Barsalou and Wiemer-Hastings 2005), and more emotions (e.g., Kousta et al. 2011).

3.3.1 Situations and Introspective Properties

Barsalou and Wiemer Hastings (2005) demonstrated that abstract concepts focus on situations and on introspective properties. They presented participants with three abstract ("freedom," "truth," and "invention"), three concrete ("bird," "sofa," and "car") and three intermediate concepts ("cook," "farm," "carpet"), and asked them to produce characteristics of each concept. Each abstract and intermediate concept took three forms which were collapsed for the analyses: for example "a freedom," "to free," and "freely." Concepts were presented in isolation or preceded by a short section illustrating a situation: For example, for the concept "truth," the situation described a boy who told his mother that he had not broken a vase, and his mother believing him. Results showed that both concrete and abstract concepts were grounded in situations. However, compared to concrete concepts, which activate the physical aspects of situations, abstract concepts focus "on the social, event, and introspective aspects of situations (e.g., people, communication, beliefs, and complex relations)." (p. 152). In a further feature generation task, Wiemer-Hastings and Xu (2005) found with a larger sample of concepts that the concrete ones elicited more item properties, while abstract concepts evoked more introspective properties. They also found that while both concrete and abstract concepts were grounded in situations, they relied on different aspects of situations, since abstract concepts focused more on the social aspects of situations than concrete concepts. Further evidence favoring the idea according to which abstract concepts activate situations has been collected by King (2013). Participants were presented with short scenarios, and later, they were required to perform a lexical decision task on a target abstract word. Results showed that, even if in the scenario no associate word to the target was present, the context had different impact on different kinds of abstract concepts: The scenario facilitated processing of relational abstract concepts (e.g., "ignore," which describes an act, an actor, a patient being ignored, but no internal feeling), while it did not influence activation of mental states (e.g., "depressed," which does not expresses relations but refers to a feeling).

The relevance Barsalou and Wiemer-Hastings ascribe to the relation between abstract concepts and situations is partially in line with the original idea on which the contextual availability theory (Schwanenflugel et al. 1988) is based. According to CAT, concrete concepts are strongly related to a small number of contexts, while abstract concepts are weakly related to a high number of contexts. This disparity would account for the processing advantage of concrete over abstract concepts and is supported by evidence showing that the concreteness effect disappears when contexts are provided.

However, Connell and Lynott (2012) recently found that concepts with high perceptual strength, typically assumed to be concrete, evoke a broader variety of contexts than concepts with low perceptual strength. Context diversity enhances processing rather than slowing it down.

This finding gives us some clues to interpret results showing that abstract concepts elicit more situations, as those obtained by Barsalou and Wiemer Hastings' (2005) with a feature generation task, by Roversi et al. (2013) with a feature generation task, and by Caramelli et al. (in preparation) with a definition task with the concepts "risk," "danger," and "prevention." In fact, it is possible that the number of situations produced for abstract words was higher than those produced for concrete words because in the second case more perceptual, partonomic, and taxonomic properties were produced. If this is true, this would obviously pose some problems to the theory that abstract concepts are grounded in backward situations.

However, an alternative is possible, and it relies on the role played by what Connell and Lynnot (2012) call situational complexity. As they argue, perceptual strength and situational complexity are not mutually exclusive. This position is in line with ours. Indeed, we argued that one of the characteristics of abstract concepts is that they are embedded in complex contexts and relations (see Borghi et al. 2013). Therefore, it is possible that concrete concepts are highly related to a wide variety of simple contexts, while abstract concepts are related to more complex contexts and embedded in a complex network of relations. This characteristics of abstract concepts would be able to account for the two experimental results found, that is, the fact that abstract concepts are less characterized by perceptual strength than concrete ones (Connell and Lynott 2012), and the fact that they evoke a higher number of situations (Barsalou and Wiemer-Hastings 2005; Caramelli et al. in preparation).

In sum, according to a promising view, one distinctive characteristics of abstract concepts is that they are more anchored to situations compared to concrete ones. However, the role of situations for characterizing abstract concepts should be better clarified, since so far little evidence has been provided in favor of this view, as argued by Pecher et al. (2011).

3.3.2 Emotions

A recent proposal highlights the importance of emotions in characterizing abstract concepts. We decided to insert it among the models which highlight that abstract concepts differ in content from concrete ones. However, this theory could be qualified as a hybrid model as well, since it argues that abstract concepts are characterized more by emotions and linguistic information, and concrete concepts more by sensorimotor information.

The proposal, outlined by Kousta et al. (2011; see also Kousta et al. 2009) and by Vigliocco et al. (2013a, b), rests on experimental and neural evidence. In the experimental studies, a large sample of concrete and abstract words was used, in which many lexical dimensions were controlled, among which familiarity, context availability, and imageability. Furthermore, norms on mode of acquisition (Della Rosa et al. 2010) were used. The inclusion among the norms of context availability and imageability is crucial, since two classical and influent theories of abstract concepts, the context availability theory (CAT) and the dual coding theory (DCT), rest on them, as clarified in Chap. 1. Results obtained with a lexical decision task (which implies distinguishing words from non-words) showed that, when context availability and imageability were controlled, the usual advantage in processing of concrete over abstract words (concreteness effect) was not present. Surprisingly, an opposite abstractness effect was found: Abstract concepts were processed faster than concrete ones. A regression analysis extended this result to lexical decision response times of a wide sample of words ($n = 2{,}330$). More crucially, the authors found with an experiment conducted on 430 words that the best predictor for the advantage of abstract over concrete words was emotional valence, that is, whether the words had a positive, a negative, or no emotional connotation. Controlling for valence, the advantage of abstract words disappeared. This result was recently complemented by neural evidence showing stronger activation for abstract words in the rostral anterior cingulate cortex (rACC), an area which plays a regulatory role in emotional stimuli processing (Vigliocco et al. 2013a, b). This result will be further discussed in Chap. 5
. The authors conclude that because context availability and imageability were kept constant, neither CAT nor DCT can account for their results. In addition, given that modality of acquisition was kept constant, they argue that differences in activation of linguistic information do not exhaust the difference between concrete and abstract concepts, but that emotions as well play a major role in abstract concept representation. Notice, however, that this is not the whole story: When removing the effect of valence, the advantage of abstract words was still maintained in accuracy. This could be due to the role played by linguistic information for abstract concepts.

On the basis of these data, they develop an embodied theory according to which abstract and concrete concepts differ in terms of the distribution of the experiential information which characterizes them. While concrete concepts are grounded primarily in sensorimotor information, abstract ones evoke mostly linguistic information and emotions.

A novel and interesting part of this theory is that it proposes a developmental trajectory. The authors rest on evidence showing that emotional development precedes language development and indicating that words referring to emotions are acquired rather early at around 20 months of age. They consider concreteness, valence, and age of acquisition of a large sample of 2,120 words and demonstrate that abstract words with emotional content are acquired earlier than neutral abstract words. On the basis of these data, they argue "these data are indicative of the possibility that emotion may provide a bootstrapping mechanism for the acquisition of abstract words" (Kousta et al. 2011, p. 26).

Overall, this view is supported by compelling evidence, both behavioral and neural, and it also proposes an interesting developmental course. Its main shortcoming resides in the fact that emotional words can be considered a very special kind of abstract words, as discussed in Chap. 1 and as shown also by the data by Kousta et al. (2011) on conceptual acquisition. However, this is only a partial limitation. Indeed, the proponents of this view could argue that the theory does not concern only emotional words, but it claims that valence characterizes more generally all abstract concepts (see Chap. 5 for further discussion).

The WAT proposal and this theory emphasizing the role of emotions, even if clearly different, have much in common. Both proposals highlight the fact that both concrete and abstract concepts are grounded in sensorimotor experience, but at the same time, both theories highlight the specificity of concrete and abstract concepts as well. Furthermore, both proposals underline that multiple aspects might underlie conceptual representation. But this is not the end of the story. While many theories have called attention to the primary role of linguistic information for abstract words, no theory to our knowledge has put emphasis on the importance of the social and emotional aspects linked to word acquisition. WAT attempts to emphasize the role of language considering not only the semantic and syntactic aspects, but also the pragmatics aspects (for recent evidence showing how semantics and pragmatics are strictly interwoven, see Egorova et al. 2013; Prinz 2013) and ascribing relevance also to the social context in which language is acquired. In this social context, it is likely that emotions play a major part. Therefore, the finding that emotional valence characterizes more abstract than concrete concepts is fully in line with the WAT proposal, according to which the social context of acquisition is more important for abstract than for concrete words.

3.4 Metaphors

The most influential embodied view on abstract concepts representation is the conceptual metaphor view (for a thorough overview, see Pecher et al. 2011; for a recent special issue, see Fusaroli and Morgagni 2013). This view was initially proposed in cognitive linguistics (Lakoff and Johnson 1980; Lakoff 1987; Gibbs 1994, 2005) and then extended to psychology and cognitive neuroscience. Metaphors are really pervasive in our language: For example, the metaphor "argument is war" would underlie expressions such as "He attacked every weak point in my argument," the metaphor "time is money" would underlie expressions such as "You are wasting my time" (Lakoff and Johnson 1980). The basic tenet of this view is that concrete concepts are used as metaphor (the "vehicle") in order to represent abstract concepts (the "topic"). This metaphorical process allows humans to comprehend one kind of experience on the basis of another embodied experience, which provides its structure and grounding. Different metaphors can structure a single concept and capture different aspects of it: For example, the meaning of the abstract concept "love" (the "topic") would be structured differently by different "vehicles": Love is a journey, it is madness, it is a magnetic field, etc. Spatialization is an important part of this process: For example, the embodied concept of "up" would structure many domains, such as that of hierarchy and power (power is up), that of happiness (happy is up), and others. Along the same line, Fauconnier and Turner (1998) recognize the centrality of metaphorical projection to structure our thought. According to the conceptual blending theory (Coulson 2000; Fauconnier and Turner 1998), attributes and structure from a source mental space are selected and imported into a blended space, where they can be combined with further background knowledge (see also Coulson and van Petten 2002).

The conceptual metaphor theory is supported by a variety of experimental evidence. Meier and Robinson (2004) demonstrated with linguistic stimuli that evaluations of positive words were faster when words were in the up rather than the down position, while the opposite was true for negative words. Meier et al. (2007) demonstrated that the up–down image schema affected memory of the abstract concepts related to God and Evil: People tended to encode and remember better God-like images when they were in a high position and Devil-like images when they were in a low position. Giessner and Schubert (2007) demonstrated that also the representation of power is structured by an up–down image schema: A longer vertical line increased judged power of managers compared to a shorter one, and the more one manager was presented as powerful, the higher they tended to locate his/her box in an organization chart. This up–down organization seems to structure the representation of the concept of power overall, and it does not intervene only in the selection of response phase. Thus, the up–down image schema represents the background structure of a variety of abstract concepts, such as those of affect (positive up, negative down), divinity, and power.

In a similar vein, Boot and Pecher (2010) showed that the abstract notion of "similarity" relies on the concrete concept of "closeness." Participants determined whether two squares, located at a different spatial distance, were similar or not in color. Performance with similar color was better when the squares were closer, with dissimilar color when they were farther from each other.

Boot and Pecher (2011) demonstrated that the abstract concept of "category" is grounded in the concept of "container." Importantly, in many of these studies, the authors decided to avoid using linguistic stimuli in order to demonstrate that conceptual mapping effects pertain concepts and not only word meanings since they exist beyond language.

Probably the domain which has been more thoroughly investigated in order to support the conceptual metaphor theory concerns the relationship between space and time (for a recent review, see Bonato et al. 2012; see Chap. 6 for discussion). The underlying idea is that the abstract concept of time would be structured thanks to the concrete notion of space. Researchers started by considering that the relationship between space and time is asymmetrical: For example, we often rely on space when talking about time (e.g., we say "a long holiday"). Boroditsky and Ramscar (2002) showed with ingenious experiments that people in an ego-moving perspective (for example, people at the beginning of a train journey, people who had just flown in, or people who were at the beginning of a lunch line) tended to respond to an ambiguous time question producing an ego-moving response. When required to process the sentence "next Wednesday's meeting has been moved forward two days," they interpreted forward as after (i.e., Friday). In contrast, people in a time-moving perspective (for example, people who were at the end of the trip, or of the line) tended to refer forward to earlier (i.e., Wednesday). This result indicates that time and space are strictly interwoven and suggests that thinking about time is grounded in embodied experience. Casasanto and Boroditsky (2008) showed that, when providing judgments about time, people are not able to ignore spatial information, while the opposite is not true. For example, participants were required to estimate line length and duration: Even when required to estimate duration, they were unable to ignore spatial information on line length, but the interference did not work in the other way round. Results confirmed an asymmetrical dependence of time upon space: Distance affected duration estimates more than duration affected distance estimates. The fact that the task did not involve linguistic stimuli or response led the authors to argue that the metaphorical relation between time and space extends beyond language.

Flusberg et al. (2010) designed a connectionist model showing that the way we think about the abstract concept of time is grounded on our online representations of space. The model accounts for a number of results collected in Boroditsky's laboratory. Flusberg et al. show that this grounding is not due to the fact that space and time are typically experienced together, but to the structural similarity between time and space; thus, they showed that the neural network progressively learned to map the directionality of time (from early to late) with the directionality of space (from west to east).

The examples we provided are only a few, but the conceptual metaphor theory, and specifically the idea that the notion of time is understood referring to the concept of space, is supported by a lot of evidence. However, it has been also subject of much criticism. In our opinion, one of the most effective critiques to the view according to which thinking about time is grounded on the more concrete experience of space is advanced by Kranjec and Chatterjee (2010) in a recent paper. The authors outline two problems. The first is theoretical: According to them, the notion of spatial schema is a theoretical construct, representing a mediation between perception and language; thus, it is not necessarily "embodied" in a strong sense. The second problem is empirical: They point out that the evidence in favor of the conceptual metaphor theory is mainly linguistic and behavioral, but that neural evidence on the relationships between space and time is lacking. In analyzing the literature, the authors argue that the idea that time is grounded in spatial representation has often led researchers to neglect the importance of time. Time is the most frequently used noun in English; in addition, temporal language appears earlier in the development: The frequency and early acquisition of temporal notions suggest that spatial grounding is not necessary for time representation. Moreover, in the brain, different mechanisms and areas, both subcortical and cortical, represent different kinds of temporal information. Thus, according to Kranjec and Chatterjee (2010), it might be unnecessary to assume that time is grounded in space, given that dedicated neural circuits for time do exist. However, it is also possible that time is grounded both in spatial abstractions and directly in timing areas: As recognized by the authors, the two hypotheses are not necessarily mutually exclusive.

The theory of conceptual mapping is probably the most influential embodied theory of abstract concepts, and there is compelling evidence in its favor, as we have seen thanks to the reported examples. However, various problems remain open (see Pecher et al. 2011).

Recently, a study challenged the postulate of CMT of an unidirectional influence from sensorimotor experience to metaphors, and not viceversa (Slepian and Ambady 2014). Participants learned new metaphors concerning weight and time; later, they were to provide weight estimates of old and of new books. If exposed to the metaphor that the past is heavy, they tended to perceive as heavier old books, if they had been exposed to the metaphor that the present is heavy, they perceived as heavier a book seemingly from the present. These results indicate that novel metaphors can influence sensorimotor processes as well, thus leading to a bidirectional influence between metaphors and sensorimotor states. This evidence requires at a minimum that the conceptual metaphor theory is extended to account for the bidirectional relationship between metaphors and sensorimotor processing.

Further problems of the CMT have been raised by different authors. One debated issue concerns whether metaphorical grounding is necessary in order to understand abstract concepts, or whether accessing to metaphors might simply occur in certain cases. Evidence indicates that, at least in some subdomains, metaphors are automatically activated. However, this does not imply that without metaphors, the comprehension process would be impaired (for a similar objection against embodied cognition evidence more generally, see Mahon and Caramazza 2008). One way to address this claim (even if not completely) may consist in demonstrating that image schemas activation anticipates full comprehension of abstract concepts. Another more convincing way to address this claim is based on research on patients who have lost semantic knowledge of concrete concepts: Are they still able to understand abstract concepts? The absence of evidence in both directions has led some researchers (e.g., Murphy 1996; Pecher et al. 2011) to refuse the strong version proposed by Lakoff and Johnson, according to which abstract concepts' representation is structured thanks to the concrete concepts on which they are metaphorically grounded, and to endorse instead a weak version: Both concepts would have a structured representation, and the representation of the concrete concept (e.g., space) would influence that of the abstract one (e.g., time).

A second problem of the conceptual metaphor view is that a consistent part of the evidence obtained relies on linguistic stimuli. However, there might be important differences between linguistic metaphors and underlying and more basic representation of the relationship between items. For example, using linguistic stimuli, Casasanto (2008) found that pairs of abstract concepts were judged more similar when the stimuli were closer together, in line with the idea that "similarity is closeness," while when providing perceptual judgments closer stimuli were judged to be less similar. To cope with this problem, many recent studies have shown that the conceptual metaphor theory does not pertain linguistic but conceptual relations.

One further limitation of this view is that the neural evidence is still lacking. As argued by Kranjec and Chatterijee with regard to the relationship between space and time, it is unclear why the neural regions dedicated to time processing would not be activated during comprehension of time concepts.

Another problem of the conceptual metaphor view (see Dove 2009, for such a critique) is that its developmental trajectory is not plausible (Murphy 2006). Children start indeed to use metaphors rather late (Winner et al. 1976). A further problem highlighted by Barsalou and Wiemer-Hastings (2005) is that it can provide only a partial account of abstractness. Metaphors might take part in the representation of abstract concepts, but this is not necessarily the case. More crucially, the meaning of abstract concepts is not fully exhausted by metaphors: Metaphors might render some of their aspects more salient, but direct experiencing the referents of abstract concepts is crucial for their meaning.

Finally, we see one limit that the conceptual metaphor view shares with the action-based theory of abstract concepts, and that does not appear to be easily solvable with further evidence. It concerns its generalizability. In fact, it is hard to imagine how far this evidence can be extended beyond specific domains (for a similar critique, see Dove 2009; Goldman and De Vignemont 2009). How could we ground "philosophy," or "truth," in metaphors?

3.5 Multiple Representation View

In the previous sections, we have reviewed embodied theories according to which abstract and concrete concepts do not differ as they are both grounded in action, and embodied theories that, even if maintaining an embodied stance, highlight possible differences in grounding and representing concrete and abstract words.

In this section, we will distinguish our proposal from similar views. We will focus on proposals that share with WAT the idea that knowledge is represented by multiple systems, based on sensorimotor and on linguistic experience (see also Andrews et al. 2009, 2013).

3.5.1 Representational Pluralism: Dove

Dove (2009)'s view departs from an embodied stance, as it qualifies as only partially embodied—Dove (2011) entitles his Frontiers paper "On the need for embodied and dis-embodied cognition", and it heavily rests on Paivio's (1971, 1986) view. Dove (2009) argues that concepts are couched in two different types of representations, modal, and amodal, both perceptual and not perceptual. He recognizes that much evidence favoring an embodied approach has been collected, but this evidence is confined to highly imageable and concrete concepts. He argues that abstract concepts might be grounded in metaphors—for example, the concept of "respect" can involve a vertical metaphor—but this does not exhaust the conceptual content. According to him, the weakness of embodied approaches with respect to abstract concepts is not confined to the collected evidence, but it extends to the theories, which are built to explain concrete concepts and are much more compelling with them (see his critiques to the proposal by Jesse Prinz). Once highlighted the weakness of embodied theoretical accounts of abstract concepts, Dove argues that some abstract concepts imply amodal representations. Specifically, he relies heavily on studies in cognitive neuroscience and neuropsychology, which propose a novel Paivian dual code account, that is, which explain imageability effects on the basis of multiple semantic codes. Dove (2011) goes one step further, as he claims: "The core thesis of this paper is that concepts are couched in two types of simulation-based representations: those associated with non-linguistic experience of the world and those associated with experience of language."

As recognized by Dove, his view partially overlaps with the WAT proposal: We argue that concrete and abstract concepts are grounded in both sensorimotor and linguistic experience, but that the acquisition of concrete concepts depends more on direct sensorimotor experience and the acquisition of abstract concepts is more likely to depend on linguistic experience. Dove explains that his proposal differs from WAT as in his view, the acquisition of language creates an amodal, disembodied system, since "natural language on my view is not merely another source of information about the world but is also another way of thinking about the world…. language is an internalized amodal symbol system that is built on an embodied substrate. As such, it extends our cognitive reach and helps us overcome the problem of abstraction" (Dove 2011, p. 8). In a more recent paper, the view outlined by Dove (2013) becomes closer to ours, as he speaks of language as an "embodied representation system" that interacts with other embodied systems, and he underlines that the abilities acquired thanks to language allow to use it not only as a medium of communication but also of thought.

We agree with Dove that evidence on abstract concepts is still not sufficient and, as we detailed above, we share his concern that not only the evidence but also some theoretical embodied proposals on abstract concepts fall short as they, even if interesting, are too limited in scope and therefore not able to provide a comprehensive account of abstractness. The proposal advanced by Dove and the WAT proposal share many aspects, and the common elements increase if we consider the last version of Dove's proposal (Dove 2013). Some of the evidence we collected is clearly in favor of a multiple representation approach (e.g., Scorolli et al. 2011, 2012) (see Fig. 3.3), and WAT can be considered as a multimodal approach.

Still, the constructive part of Dove's proposal departs from the WAT view, for at least two reasons.

The first difference between Dove's approach and WAT is his defense of amodal symbols. We fully agree with him that the internalized language can be used to improve thought processes. But we do not share Dove's view that this language we use to think would be amodal. According to the EG perspective, language is grounded in perception, action, and emotional systems, thus it is not amodal. We see profound differences between the view, initially proposed by Vygotsky, later adopted and developed by some philosophers claiming an extended mind view (e.g., Clark 2008) and that we share (e.g., Borghi and Cimatti 2010; Borghi et al. 2013), that internalized language can be used as an instrument for thought which augments our computational abilities (see also Mirolli and Parisi 2009) and the idea of an amodal, arbitrary language of thought: The latter does not correspond to the real language we use, but it would be the product of a transduction process, which so far has not been empirically demonstrated (for compelling critiques of this amodal view, promoted for example by Fodor 1975, see Barsalou 1999). Notice, however, that, in a recent paper, Dove (2013) seems to slightly change or to better clarify his position: He does not speak any more of disembodiment but argues that his view is compatible with a weakly embodied approach. Again, however, he stresses the role played by language in terms with which we only partially agree: "If the underlying cognitive system is not inherently symbolic, then the acquisition of a natural language may provide a means of extending our computational power by giving us access to a new type of representational format." We agree with Dove that language modifies our categories. However, we tend to avoid ascribing certain characteristics, as productivity and combinatorial capacity, only to language and not to other more basic cognitive processes as well. In line with theories of reuse (Anderson 2010; Gallese 2008; Parkinson and Wheatley 2013), we believe that some basic structures and mechanisms, as those of the motor system, are reused at a higher level by language: In this very sense, we can speak of language grounding (Borghi 2012 investigates this issue in more details). This does not mean that language use does not introduce modifications and changes in previously formed and more ancient structures, as those of the motor system. However, some characteristics of productivity and combinatorial capacity are possessed by the motor system as well as studies on the "motor vocabulary" reveal (Fogassi et al. 2005; Rizzolatti et al. 1988; Gentilucci and Rizzolatti 1988). For example, Gentilucci and Rizzolatti (1988) and Rizzolatti et al. (1988) introduced the metaphor of a motor vocabulary to refer to the neurons of area F5 in the monkey's brain: The "words" of this vocabulary are neurons connected to different motor acts, which can be hierarchically organized: Some refer to the goal of an action (e.g., grasping, holding), some to phases in which the action can be segmented (hand aperture phase), and some to the posture with

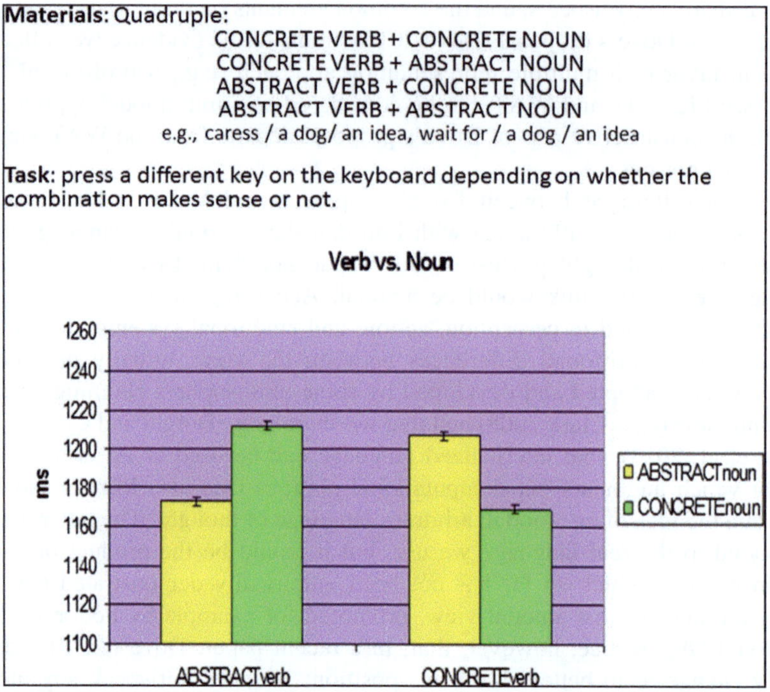

Fig. 3.3 Study by Scorolli et al. (2011). German and Italian participants had to respond by pressing a different key on the keyboard whether noun–verb combinations made sense or not. Combinations were composed by abstract/concrete verbs and abstract/concrete nouns. The interaction reported on the graph shows that compatible combinations (abstract–abstract and concrete–concrete) are faster than mixed combinations. The result is in line with multiple representation views, according to which abstract and concrete words are processed in parallel systems (linguistic and sensorimotor), so that costs of processing within the same system are the lowest. The result was replicated and extended in a TMS study by Scorolli et al. (2012). The same stimuli and paradigm were also used in the Sakreida et al. (2013) fMRI study, reported in Chap. 5

which an action can be executed (e.g., precision grip). These studies suggest that, similarly to words, motor acts can be combined in novel ways (even if obviously they are not arbitrarily linked to their referents, as words are). As clarified by Barsalou (1999), the productivity and combinatorial properties of symbols do not characterize only amodal symbols but grounded symbols as well. In sum, we are with Dove as he highlights the potentiality of language, but we do not think that language provides a novel representational format.

The second difference between Dove's view and WAT concerns his defense of an approach, which for many aspects relies on Paivio's (1986) DCT. Dove's view departs from DCT in that he proposes that perceptual symbols rather than mental images are the basic units of both verbal and non-verbal representations. However, much of the evidence he reports in support of his proposal, both behavioral and neuroscientific, relies on the important role of imageability; thus, it has the shortcoming we discussed in the introduction: Imageability cannot be conflated with concreteness, and imageability ratings cannot explain perceptual strength as they are profoundly biased toward vision.

3.5.2 Grounding and Sign Tracking: Jesse Prinz

Prinz (2002, 2012) is a philosopher who proposes a theory of abstract concepts that has a lot in common with the WAT view. We will outline it, and then, we will discuss some criticisms Dove advanced to it, and finally, we will identify similarities and differences between this theory and the WAT view.

Prinz (2005) provocatorily claims that the explanation of abstract concept is a challenge for traditional disembodied theories, rather than for embodied ones: "If concepts were amodal, we wouldn't face the question of how we can depict democracy, but we would face an equally challenging question. How can an arbitrary amodal symbol inside the head represent democracy? How can it represent anything at all?" (Prinz 2005, p. 12). Understanding words requires a tracking strategy: Since they are arbitrary symbols, to get their meaning, they need to be anchored to something non-verbal. Abstract categories are typically correlated with features that can be perceived and that can work as signs for the category. The "sign tracking" strategy consists in "representing such categories by detecting contingently correlated perceivable features" (Prinz 2002, p. 169).

According to the author, a first way to comprehend abstract concepts is to ground them in concrete scenarios. For example, "justice" can be grasped referring to simple situations: Inequality can be simulated referring to a scenario in which a person gets two cookies, and another three. Even if grounding, or sign tracking, holds for many abstract concepts, Prinz recognizes that it might not suffice for all kinds of concepts. He therefore identifies several further ways by which perceptual symbols can explain abstract concepts representation: metaphorical projection, mental operations and emotional connotations, and labeling. Beyond sign tracking, we will consider only the strategies referring to internal perceptual states and to labeling; we have discussed the metaphorical projection strategy elsewhere, since it is part of structured theories. According to Prinz (2002, 2005, 2012), abstract concepts evoke internal perceptual states (see also Barsalou and Wiemer-Hastings 2005, according to whom beyond situations introspective properties would characterize abstract concepts), particularly emotions. For example, the notion of "meaningful activity" is understood through introspection of motivations and of emotions. It is possible, however, that logical abstract concepts such as "truth" or "identity" are not understood through emotions. One further strategy proposed by Prinz (2002) is the labeling one: For example, the concept of "democracy" would be comprehended in terms of a network of associated terms. We will discuss the advantages of this strategy when we will outline distributional approaches. The novelty is that these associated terms are real words, not amodal symbols. Prinz (2005) states that this strategy is not sufficient per se, however. We do need to ground labels in order to understand them. This is exactly in line with our view: Abstract concepts need to be grounded in sensorimotor system; at the same time, they activate associate words more than concrete concepts do.

Dove (2009) criticizes the different points of the proposal by Jesse Prinz. We will report his critiques, clarifying whether and how they depart from our view. First of all, Dove (2009) criticizes the view, according to which abstract concepts are represented through the simulation of people performing the actions typically associated to a given concept. He uses as an example the concept of "democracy." Dove argues that, given that the representation cannot be really fine-grained due to cognitive load problems, it necessarily has to take into account more typical actions associated with democracy. This would leave it unclear to what extent a representation based on perceptual symbols would have advantages over an amodal one, since a proper tracking strategy cannot be defined. But, as we discussed in Chap. 1, all concepts, even subordinate ones, always imply some degree of abstraction: The category of siamese cats abstracts from single instances of siamese cats as Peg, Fufi, etc. Thus, the capability of tracking differs only in terms of degree between concrete and abstract concepts. In addition, it is unclear to us why and where Dove puts a border between concrete and abstract terms. His argument, that given the conceptual complexity of certain notions only a subset of elements would be considered, holds also for concrete terms, which can be rather complex and the representation of which may vary consistently depending on the expertise: Consider for example complex artifacts such as robots and computers, or consider how complex the "concrete" living beings are.

The strategy based on internal states and emotions is also criticized by Dove, who uses the notion of "democracy" as an example to counterargument to Prinz: "Genuine acts of voting are not distinguished from false ones by the emotion experienced by the voters at the time of voting." Here, we agree with Dove; however, in his recent book "Beyond human nature," Jesse Prinz does not use "democracy" to give an example of the simulation of events using introspections or motivation; rather, he clarifies that a notion such as "democracy" can be understood referring to a variety of procedures we typically experience which involve counting votes, as for example, when we are with our family and have to decide where to eat dinner tonight.

As to the labeling strategy, according to Dove (2009), it has the problem of individuating in a precise way which associations pertain the conceptual content and which do not. In addition, he argues that a labeling strategy cannot explain polysemy and synonymy. As argued elsewhere, however (Borghi and Cimatti 2012), anchoring words to the way we use them can represent the solution of the problem. Indeed, polysemic words and synonyms are related to different, but similar, experiences, both linguistic and sensorimotor.

In sum, we think that the view proposed by Prinz (2002, 2012) has a lot of potentialities, and in many respects, it converges with the WAT proposal. The view that abstract concepts are grounded in concrete scenarios is shared by most embodied theories, including WAT. The emotional strategy is interesting as well.

According to the WAT proposal, abstract concepts imply a social kind of acquisition; the social aspects, even if present, are typically less prominent in the representation of concrete concepts and in their acquisition. These social aspects might well include some emotional counterparts, given the strong associations between sociality and emotions (see the section on emotions). One further point is relevant in this proposal. According to Prinz, a concept such as democracy would be grasped both through mental imagery and through verbal skills, used to track definitions used by other authoritative members of our community. Comprehending abstract concepts implies the simple capacity "to match mental images with reality and sentences with testimony" (Prinz 2012). This view, according to which we rely on testimony to get the conceptual gist, converges with the idea proposed by WAT and discussed in Chaps. 2 and 4 of the importance of language and in particular of explanations for abstract concepts.

WAT diverges from Prinz's proposal in some aspects that can be considered as minor. First, Prinz highlights the role of mental imagery and of perception for conceptual representation, while WAT underlines more the importance of the motor system and of action. However, as argued elsewhere (Borghi 2005; Borghi and Caruana in press), no real dichotomy between embodied and grounded theories emphasizing more the role of perception or of action exists. Second, WAT extends Prinz's view by proposing that words are tools, that is, not mere vehicles of pre-existing experiences but also actions/experiences in their own right. Finally, WAT underlines the peculiar role played by acquisition in determining the representation of both concrete and abstract concepts.

3.5.3 Hybrid Models: Distributional and Embodied Approaches

Recent literature shows a flourishing increase of hybrid models. Embodied and distributional approaches are often divided by disciplinary boundaries, as recently explained by Andrews et al. (2013). While embodied approaches are mostly widespread in cognitive science and neuroscience, distributional and statistical accounts are more popular in computer science and modeling. In distributional views, meaning derives from the relationship between a word and its associate words, not between a word and its referent: As nicely summarized by Firth (1957), "You shall know a word by the company it keeps" (p. 11). According to one of the earliest and most powerful models, the latent semantic analysis (LSA) (Landauer and Dumais 1997), word meaning derives from the statistical co-occurrence of words in large text corpora. This distributive information is able to account for many empirical findings, most notably of semantic priming. Statistical learning theories are interesting also due to their anti-nativist flavor, since they ascribe a major role to linguistic experience. They are interesting, for us, also because statistical learning promoters do not defend Fodor's ideas of amodal mental words, which are the product of a transduction from sensorimotor to simil-linguistic features. Rather, meaning is captured by the associations and the relations between real words. Andrews et al. (2013) show in a comprehensive review how attempts to reconcile the embodied and distributional approaches are starting to emerge in philosophy, psychology, computer science, and cognitive neuroscience. Our view is completely in line with this reconciliatory proposal. However, we believe that probably reconciling the two approaches is not sufficient to fully explain meaning, and particularly, meaning of abstract words. We will detail the reasons why we think this is not the whole story while analyzing in detail one influent hybrid approach, the symbol interdependency hypothesis proposed by Max Louwerse and collaborators.

3.5.3.1 Symbol Interdependency Hypothesis: Louwerse

Louwerse and Jeuniaux (2008) (see also Louwerse 2011) recently proposed the symbol interdependency hypothesis, according to which language comprehension is both embodied and symbolic. Notice that the theory they propose concerns conceptual representation overall, and does not focus on abstract concepts and words. However, from this general theory, a view on abstract concepts can be derived. The core of their proposal lies in the argument that symbols "can, but do not always have to, be grounded". Specifically, they propose that, since language captures and keep track of the embodied relations that occur in the world, it can provide a "shortcut to the embodied relations in the world". Indeed, symbols—for example words—are interdependent and interconnected with other symbols, but also with objects, that is, their referents. This characteristic guarantees the possibility that not all symbols are necessarily grounded: Some symbols are grounded, while others are grounded through the mediation of other symbols. The combination of an embodied and a symbolic approach would allow our conceptual system to be more efficient and to store and retrieve information in a more economical way. According to EG views, it would not be economical to transduce perceptual and action information into amodal symbols (Barsalou 1999). In the same vein, according to the SIH, it would not be convenient to transduce words into modality specific states. In support of their theory, L&J revise existing evidence. They argue that, for tasks implying deep semantic processing, the evidence favoring embodied account is rather uncontroversial. The story is different, however, for tasks that involve superficial semantic processing, such as semantic decision tasks, due to the fact that no transduction in a code other than the linguistic one, that is, no direct grounding, is necessary. Besides evidence favoring an embodied approach, according to them, there is evidence that symbols can derive meanings on the basis of their relationships with other amodal symbols. In particular, models such as LSA (Landauer and Dumais 1997) and Hyperspace Analogue to Language (HAL, Burgess and Lund 1997) determine the semantic relatedness among different text units (words, texts, etc.) analyzing the frequency of their co-occurrences and the similarity of the contexts in which they co-occur.

According to these models, the meaning of a word such as "bird" would be the product of statistical computations from associations between "bird" and other concepts such as "nest, beak, fly, and robin." These models produce outputs that correlate with behavioral results, in particular with semantic priming results, in explaining figurative language (for an overview, see Louwerse 2011).

Evidence in favor of the SIH was recently collected by Louwerse and collaborators. For example, Louwerse and Jeuniaux (2010) presented participants with words arranged either according to an iconic relation (e.g., the word "attic" was displayed above the word "basement" on the computer screen) or a reverse-iconic relation (the word "basement" was presented above the word "attic") (Zwaan and Yaxley 2003). They found that linguistic factors, such as the word order frequency, better predicted results obtained in semantic judgments for words, while embodiment factors, such as the iconicity ratings, better predicted results obtained in iconicity judgments for pictures. Louwerse and Connell (2011) compared the embodied/modal and the statistical approach in predicting the perceptual modalities of words. They found that the modal approach was more precise, since the finer distinctions between auditory, gustatory, haptic, olfactory, and visual modalities were provided, while the statistical approach was not able to differentiate between olfactory and gustatory modalities. Louwerse and Connell performed an experiment in which they replicated the task designed by Pecher et al. (2003), in which participants had to verify whether a property is true or false of a given item. Two consecutive properties could be of the same modality (e.g., both visual) or of different modalities, thus determining a shift, for example from the auditory to the tactile modality. L&C operationalized the embodied shift as the shift between the five perceptual modalities (visual, haptic, auditory, olfactory, and gustatory modality), the statistics shift as between three linguistic modalities (visual–haptic, auditory, olfactory–gustatory). They found that the statistical approach better predicts faster responses, the embodied approach slower responses. The authors interpret their results as support for the LIH and for the LASS theory (Barsalou et al. 2008), claiming that less precise linguistic processes occur earlier than more detailed simulation processes. Connell and Lynott (2013) recently demonstrated that people tend to use linguistic shortcut to decide whether a combination between concepts will be coherent not only for shallow tasks, as sensibility judgments, but also for tasks involving deep conceptual processing, as the feature generation tasks. Further recent evidence has been found in support of the distributional approach in a variety of domains: For example, Hutchinson and Louwerse (in press) found that the statistical approach is able to account for the SNARC effect, that is, for the finding that left-hand responses to parity judgments are faster with smaller than with larger numbers, while the result is opposite with right-hand responses.

The evidence we illustrated testifies that the statistical account is rather powerful in predicting results. However, it cannot predict the results at the same level of detail as the embodied simulation account. In our opinion, this demonstrates that grounding of concepts is important for full comprehension. As to results on timing, we will discuss them when we deal with the LASS theory, for which they are directly relevant. One further limitation, which is crucial in the context of this book, is that the evidence collected so far concerns only concrete concepts and not abstract ones.

In evaluating the theory as a whole, we think that the part in which it critiques the embodied view has some limitations, but the proposal has many reasons of interest and many similarities with our view. First, we do not think it is true that most evidence on language grounding is obtained with deep processing tasks. A paradigmatic example is given by the work of Pulvermüller and other authors who demonstrated that the motor system is activated very quickly and with tasks that imply shallow semantic processing such as lexical decision tasks. In addition, even studies performed with tasks that require deep semantic processing typically focused on dimensions that were not relevant to the task. For example, Stanfield and Zwaan (2001) found faster responses when sentences like "The ranger saw the eagle in the sky" were followed by a picture displaying a bird with outstretched wings rather than a bird in its nest: Even if the task implied deep semantic processing, the perceptual dimension of shape was automatically evoked during this task. Second, Louwerse and Jeniaux (see also Louwerse 2008) report that some spatial relations such as the upper-lower part structure which are present in the world are also present in the linguistic structure. We do not believe that the very fact that certain kinds of relations, such as the spatial ones, are encoded in language, goes against embodied theories. On the contrary, this finding might contribute to demonstrate that the argument of a complete arbitrariness of language is not completely viable and that the language structure reflects the structure of our experience. We appreciate the fact that Louwerse and Jeniaux ascribe relevance to the real language and to the associations formed between words (see Landauer and Dumais 1997, for a similar position: Knowledge is not represented by amodal symbols, but by statistical distribution of real words). However, at the same time, we believe that meaning cannot be fully explained by word associations and that some form of symbol grounding (e.g., an embodied simulation) is needed for comprehension (Harnad 1990; Cangelosi and Harnad 2000; Pezzulo and Castelfranchi 2007). In our view, both concrete and abstract words are grounded. Thus, both the concrete word "tablecloth" and the abstract word "freedom" would activate a network of associated words, but also a variety of experiences (e.g., flying, running on the grass). But the role of words would be more relevant for the second, given that the objects, situations, and experiences evoked by a label are more diverse than those kept together by the word "tablecloth."

In addition, the L&J proposal does not consider some important characteristics of language, such as its social aspect and its power in modifying cognition. The social aspects characterizing language, the fact that it is acquired through a form of social embodiment, are only partially explained by the fact that the relations between words reflect socially determined rules—language is learned in an embodied context in which different organisms interact and resonate. Furthermore, L&J do not say anything on the power words have in modifying cognition. One example of such power is given by the role language plays in categorization: Verbal labels can limit the boundaries of previously acquired categories, render them more uniform and lead speakers to converge on a subset of common features (see for example Puglisi et al. 2008). Finally, L&J do not address the issue of the role public words might play as external devices that guide our thought processes. In order to capture the complexity of language use, all these aspects should be considered; therefore, we think that the proposal by L&J should at a minimum be extended to take into account all of them.

3.5.3.2 Language and Situated Simulation (LASS) Theory: Barsalou et al.

One important view with which our proposal shares many similarities is the language and situated simulation (LASS) Theory advanced by Barsalou and collaborators (Barsalou et al. 2008; Simmons et al. 2008). Barsalou et al. (2008) propose that multiple systems underlie knowledge in the brain. LASS focuses on two of these forms of knowledge: linguistic forms (not amodal symbols!) and situated simulations. These two systems underlie concepts representation and processing and are in continuous and dynamical interaction; they are not incapsulated or modular. The LASS theory outlines how the dynamic of the process would occur and delineates the time course of activation of the two systems. Here is how the LASS proponents describe this interactive process. In linguistic tasks, the activation of linguistic forms would peak earlier, even if both the linguistic and the simulation systems are active. This would happen in line with the encoding specificity principle (Tulving and Thomson 1973), according to which memory is most effective when information available at encoding is also present at retrieval. After word recognition, further linguistic forms would be activated, at first through the simpler mechanism underlying conceptual processing, that is, word associations. These associations allow situating the cue-word within a linguistic context, and this permits to execute a variety of tasks. An important assumption of the LASS theory is that, to accomplish some tasks, such as the lexical decision tasks, that requires distinguishing words from non-words, only shallow processing is needed, and no access to deep conceptual knowledge is required. In this respect, the LASS theory is indebted to Glaser's (1992) lexical hypothesis, according to which the advantage of pictures over words is due to the fact that images access in a straightforward way the conceptual system, while words do not. Once recognized, however, the word starts activating simulations as well, and it allows accessing to conceptual meaning in order to prepare for situated actions. In this case, the word works as a "pointer." According to the authors, even if the activation of simulations can be rather fast and occur automatically, for many seconds, it does not dominate the initial stages of word processing. This idea is difficult to reconcile with Pulvermueller's et al. (2005) results, showing that meaning of words such as "kick," "lick," and "pick" activate in a somatotopic way the motor cortex about 150 ms after word presentation. To conciliate their view with Pulvermueller's, the authors propose that "simulations are likely to be activated simultaneously while the executive system is producing responses from the linguistic system" (Barsalou et al. 2008, p. 4). Notice that the authors use the term "linguistic system" to refer to the system that processes linguistic form, not linguistic meaning.

This linguistic system, which has evolved later than the simulation system, basically works as a control system for manipulating simulations; thus, it does not imply access to deep conceptual information.

To note that the LASS theory has many similarities with Paivio's dual coding view. Compared to the dual coding view, however, LASS ascribes more relevance to the simulation system for abstract concepts representation, while Paivio's view attributes more relevance to the linguistic system.

An fMRI experiment by Simmons et al. (2008) represents one of the most important evidence in favor of the LASS theory. Participants were visually presented with concepts and performed a silent property generation task. In a further scanning section, they were submitted to two localizer tasks: They were asked to perform a word association task with some concepts and to imagine a situation containing the concept for other concepts. Word associations activated mostly neural areas which are typically involved in linguistic tasks, that is, left hemisphere linguistic areas, particularly Broca's area, while image simulation activated mostly bilateral posterior areas that are typically active during mental imagery. In line with the predictions of the theory, in the property generation task, the linguistic areas were active earlier, while the second were involved in the second phase of property generation. This evidence is very interesting, however, also given the scarce temporal resolution of fMRI; it should be complemented with more detailed analyses of the time course of the emergence of different kind of properties. In addition, we think it has a further problem: It basically testifies that during conceptual tasks which employ linguistic stimuli as cues, the linguistic system is the first to be activated, while the imagery system is activated later. This does not imply at all that meaning is not accessed from very early phases. Indeed, word generation tasks, which involve activation of Broca's area, imply accessing linguistic meaning. Furthermore, notice that the Broca's area is considered the human homolog of the F5 area in monkey's brain, where mirror neurons are found (see Rizzolatti and Craighero 2004, for a review). Activation of this area could also imply an activation of the motor system to prepare for situated action. In line with this hypothesis, many studies report Broca's area activation for example during motor imagery (Binkofski et al. 2000) or during processing of action concepts disregarding the modality (vision or language) (Baumgaertner et al. 2007).

Notice that the LASS theory concerns word and conceptual processing and representation overall, and it is not focused on abstract concepts. However, Barsalou et al. (2008) report an fMRI study conducted on abstract concepts (see also Wilson-Mendenhall et al. 2014). Participants were presented with an abstract word (e.g., "convince") and asked to verify whether it applied to a picture (e.g., a politician speaking) presented after. The results showed that the brain areas related to the content of the word were active, while there was no difference in activation of linguistic areas for concrete and abstract words. The authors conclude that "the representation of abstract concepts can differentially recruit the language and simulation systems. When task conditions allow, as in previous experiments, participants rely only on the language system, because it is adequate for task performance (e.g., in lexical decision and synonym tasks). When task conditions require deeper conceptual processing, participants rely on the simulation system, because it provides the necessary information for performing the task (e.g., verifying that an abstract concept applies to a picture.... different mixtures of the language and simulation systems support the processing of abstract concepts under different task conditions" (Barsalou et al. 2008, p. 267). This evidence captures one aspect which is important for the WAT view as well: The fact that not only concrete but also abstract words are grounded. In addition, it highlights the flexibility of the human conceptual system, emphasizing its task dependency. However, we think that something is missing here: Processing a word in order to verify its relation to an image differs from processing a word in the context of other words, and this control situation was not present. Finally, it should be clearer which abstract concepts the authors selected, since for many abstract concepts, it is not easy to form mental images without any cue (e.g., "truth").

Overall, the WAT view shares with the LASS theory the idea that multiple systems represent knowledge. The main difference between our proposal and LASS lies in a different evaluation of the role played by language. The authors claim "language plays central roles in cognition and conceptualization. Nevertheless, experience plays a role that is at least as central" (Barsalou et al. 2008, p. 276). In disagreement with this, we believe that language and experience cannot be contrasted. In our view, perception-action and linguistic experiences do not have a different status. Words do not carry meaning only when they work as pointers. Instead, language carries meaning, which can be transmitted either pointing to referents in the world or referring to other words through a network of associates. One of the advantages of distributional models is that they have highlighted this very fact, allowing us to depart from the view according to which words are only pointers to their referents. Production of word associations is, in our view, a way to access to meaning. We agree that the role and weight of the linguistic and simulation systems might vary depending on the task. Without denying the profound dynamicity of our conceptual system, however, we believe that their respective weight differs also depending on the kind of concepts. As clarified more in depth elsewhere, the linguistic system is more relevant for abstract concepts, because the linguistic context was more crucial for their acquisition.

3.6 Conclusions: Many Theories, One Unifying Theory?

The aim of this chapter was to overview the most prominent recent theories seeking to account abstract concepts representations. As it appears from the discussion, the different theories capture many important aspects of abstract concepts representation. However, whether a unifying theory explaining all abstract concepts is possible is still an open issue, and we believe it is one important goal for future research.

In the overview, we have focused on embodied and on hybrid theories, and tried to show their similarities and differences from the WAT proposal. While discussing them, we have tried to demonstrate that all concepts, not only concrete ones, are grounded. We are with Prinz (2002, p. 148) as he argues: "…the failure to see how certain properties can be perceptually represented is almost always a failure of the imagination." There are indeed compelling demonstrations that abstract concepts activate the motor system, similarly to concrete ones. However, this is not the whole story. We think that the grounding of abstract concepts differs from that of concrete ones, as many authors recognize. Abstract concepts activate more situations, more linguistic information, and more emotions compared to concrete concepts, which evoke more sensorimotor information. In line with distributional models and similarly to hybrid models, the WAT proposal stresses the role of language for abstract concepts representation. However, it does not equate the role of language to the information derived from word associations in a distributed network. Certainly, linguistic experience is also that, but it goes beyond that. WAT intends language in a complex sense, as a social experience which involves our body and which triggers our emotions.

References

Anderson, M. L. (2010). Neural re-use as a fundamental organizational principle of the brain. *Behavioral and Brain Sciences, 33*, 245–266.

Andrews, M., Frank, S., & Vigliocco, G. (2013). Reconciling embodied and distributional accounts of meaning in language. *Topics in Cognitive Science.*

Andrews, M., Vigliocco, G., & Vinson, D. P. (2009). Integrating experiential and distributional data to learn semantic representations. *Psychological Review, 116*(3), 463–498.

Barsalou, L. W. (1999). Perceptual symbol systems. *Brain and Behavioural Sciences, 22*, 577–660.

Barsalou, L. W., Santos, A., Simmons, K. W., & Wilson, C. D. (2008). Language and simulations in conceptual processing. In M. De Vega, A. M. Glenberg, & A. C. Graesser (Eds.), *Symbols, embodiment and meaning* (pp. 245–283). Oxford: Oxford University Press.

Barsalou, L. W., & Wiemer-Hastings, K. (2005). Situating abstract concepts. In D. Pecher & R. Zwaan (Eds.), *Grounding cognition: The role of perception and action in memory, language, and thought* (pp. 129–163). New York: Cambridge University Press.

Baumgaertner, A., Buccino, G., Lange, R., McNamara, A., & Binkofski, F. (2007). Polymodal conceptual processing of human biological actions in the left inferior frontal lobe. *European Journal of Neuroscience, 25*(3), 881–889.

Binkofsk, F., Amunts, K., Stephan, K. M., Posse, S., Schormann, T., Freund, H. J., et al. (2000). Broca's region subserves imagery of motion: A combined cytoarchitectonic and fMRI study. *Human Brain Mapping, 11*(4), 273–285.

Bonato, M., Zorzi, M., & Umiltà, C. (2012). When time is space: Evidence for a mental time line. *Neuroscience Biobehavioral Review, 36*(10), 2257–2273.

Boot, I., & Pecher, D. (2010). Similarity is closeness: Metaphorical mapping in a perceptual task. *Quarterly Journal of Experimental Psychology, 63*, 942–954.

Boot, I., & Pecher, D. (2011). Representation of categories. *Experimental Psychology, 58*(2), 162–170.

Borghi, A. M. (2005). Object concepts and action. In D. Pecher & R. A. Zwaan (Eds.), *Grounding cognition: The role of perception and action in memory* (pp. 8–34). Cambridge: Cambridge University Press.

Borghi, A. M. (2012). Action language comprehension, affordances and goals. In Y. Coello & A. Bartolo (Eds.), *Language and action in cognitive neuroscience. Contemporary topics in cognitive neuroscience series* (pp. 125–143). Psychology Press. ISBN: 978-1-84872-082-4.

Borghi, A. M., & Caruana, F. (in press). Embodiment theories. In J. Wright (Ed.), *International encyclopedia of the social and behavioral sciences* (2nd ed.). S. Cappa (Ed.) Section of cognitive neuroscience.

Borghi, A. M., & Cimatti, F. (2010). Embodied cognition and beyond: Acting and sensing the body. *Neuropsychologia, 48*, 763–773.

Borghi, A. M., & Cimatti, F. (2012). Words are not just words: The social acquisition of abstract words. *RIFL* - ISSN: 2036-6728. doi: 10.4396/20120303

Borghi, A. M., Scorolli, C., Caligiore, D., Baldassarre, G., & Tummolini, L. (2013). The embodied mind extended: Words as social tools. *Frontiers in Psychology, 4*, 214. doi:10.3389/fpsyg.2013.00214

Boroditsky, L., & Ramscar, M. (2002). The roles of body and mind in abstract thought. *Psychological Science, 13*(2), 185–188.

Burgess, C., & Lund, K. (1997). Modeling parsing constraints with high-dimensional context space. *Language and Cognitive Processes, 12*, 177–210.

Cangelosi, A., & Harnad, S. (2000). The adaptive advantage of symbolic theft over sensorimotor toil: Grounding language in perceptual categories. *Evolution of Communication, 4*(1), 117–142.

Caramelli, N., Setti, A. & Borghi, A. M. (in preparation). How abstract is risk for workers? Expertise and contextual constraints in abstract concepts.

Casasanto, D. (2008). Similarity and proximity: When does close in space mean close in mind? *Memory and Cognition, 36*, 1047–1056.

Casasanto, D., & Boroditsky, L. (2008). Time in the mind: Using space to think about time. *Cognition, 106*, 579–593.

Chen, M., & Bargh, J. A. (1999). Consequences of automatic evaluation: Immediate behavioral predispositions to approach or avoid the stimulus. *Personality and Social Psychology Bulletin, 25*, 215–224.

Clark, A. (2008). *Supersizing the mind: Embodiment, action, and cognitive extension*. Oxford: Oxford University Press.

Connell, L., & Lynott, D. (2012). Strength of perceptual experience predicts word processing performance better than concreteness or imageability. *Cognition, 125*(3), 452–465.

Connell, L., & Lynott, D. (2013). Flexible and fast: Linguistic shortcut affects both shallow and deep conceptual processing. *Psychonomic Bulletin & Review, 20*(3), 542–550. doi:10.3758/s13423-012-0368-x

Coulson, S. (2000). *Semantic leaps: Frame-shifting and conceptual blending in meaning construction*. New York: Cambridge University Press.

Coulson, S., & Van Petten, C. (2002). Conceptual integration and metaphor: An event-related potential study. *Memory and Cognition, 30*, 958–968.

Della Rosa, P. A., Catricalà, E., Vigliocco, G., & Cappa, S. F. (2010). Beyond the abstract-concrete dichotomy: Mode of acquisition, concreteness, imageability, familiarity, age of acquisition, context availability, and abstractness norms for a set of 417 Italian words. *Behavioral Research Methods, 42*(4), 1042–1048.

Dove, G. (2009). Beyond perceptual symbols: A call for representational pluralism. *Cognition, 110*, 412–431.

Dove, G. (2011). On the need for embodied and disembodied cognition. *Frontiers in Psychology, 1*, 242. doi:10.3389/fpsyg.2010.00242

Dove, G. (2013). Thinking in words: Language as an embodied medium of thoughts. *Topics in Cognitive Science.*

Egorova, N., Shtyrov, Y., & Pulvermüller, F. (2013). Early and parallel processing of pragmatic and semantic information in speech acts: Neurophysiological evidence. *Frontiers in Human Neuroscience, 7*, 86.

Fauconnier, G., & Turner, M. (1998). Conceptual integration networks. *Cognitive Science, 22*(2), 133–187.

Firth, J. R. (1957). A synopsis of linguistic theory 1930–1955. *Studies in Linguistic Analysis (special volume of the Philological Society, Oxford)* (pp. 1–32). Oxford: Blackwell.

Fischer, M. H., & Brugger, P. (2011). When digits help digits: Spatial–numerical associations point to finger counting as prime example of embodied cognition. *Frontiers in Psychology, 2*, 260. doi:10.3389/fpsyg.2011.00260

Flusberg, S. J., Thibodeau, P. H., Sternberg, D. A., & Glick, J. J. (2010). A connectionist approach to embodied conceptual metaphor. *Frontiers in Psychology, 1*, 197. doi:10.3389/fpsyg.2010.00197

Fodor, J. A. (1975). *The language of thought*. Cambridge: Harvard University Press.

Fogassi, L., Ferrari, P. F., Gesierich, B., Rozzi, S., Chersi, F., & Rizzolatti, G. (2005). Parietal lobe: From action organization to intention understanding. *Science, 308*, 662–667.

Förster, J., & Strack, F. (1996). Influence of overt head movements on memory for valenced words: A case of conceptual-motor compatibility. *Journal of Personality and Social Psychology, 71*, 421–430.

Freina, L., Baroni, G., Borghi, A. M., & Nicoletti, R. (2009). Emotive concept-nouns and motor responses: Attraction or repulsion? *Memory & Cognition, 37*, 493–499.

Fusaroli, R., & Morgagni, S. (2013). Introduction: Thirty years later. *Journal of Cognitive Semiotics, 5*(1–2), 1–13.

Gallese, V. (2008). Mirror neurons and the social nature of language: The neural exploitation hypothesis. *Social Neuroscience, 3*, 317–333.

Gentilucci, M., & Rizzolatti, G. (1988). Cortical motor control of arm and hand movements. In M. Goodale (Ed.), *Vision and action. The control of grasping*. Norwood: Ablex.

Gianelli, C., Lugli, L., Baroni, G., Nicoletti, R., & Borghi, A. M. (2013). The impact of social context and language comprehension on behaviour: A kinematic investigation. *Plos One. 8*(12), e85151. doi: 10.1371/journal.pone.0085151.

Gibbs, R. W. J. (1994). *The poetics of mind: Figurative thought, language, and understanding*. New York: Cambridge University Press.

Gibbs, R. W. J. (2005). The psychological status of image schemas. In B. Hampe (Ed.), *From perception to meaning* (pp. 113–135). Berlin: Mouton de Gruyter.

Giessner, S. R., & Schubert, T. W. (2007). High in the hierarchy: How vertical location and judgments of leaders' power are interrelated. *Organizational Behavior and Human Decision Processes, 104*, 30–44.

Glaser, W. R. (1992). Picture naming. *Cognition, 42*, 61–105.

Glenberg, A. M., & Kaschak, M. P. (2002). Grounding language in action. *Psychonomic Bulletin & Review, 9*, 558–565.

Glenberg, A. M., Sato, M., & Cattaneo, L. (2008a). Use-induced motor plasticity affects the processing of abstract and concrete language. *Current Biology, 18*(7), R290–R291. doi:10.1016/j.cub.2008.02.036

Glenberg, A. M., Sato, M., Cattaneo, L., Riggio, L., Palumbo, D., & Buccino, G. (2008b). Processing abstract language modulates motor system activity. *Quarterly Journal of Experimental Psychology, 61*, 905–919.

Goldman, A., & de Vignemont, F. (2009). Is social cognition embodied? *Trends in Cognitive Science, 13*(4), 154–159.

Guan, C. Q., Meng, W., Yao, R., & Glenberg, A. M. (2013). Motor system contribution to the comprehension of abstract language. *PLoS ONE, 8*(9), e75183. doi:10.1371/journal.pone.0075183

Harnad, S. (1990). The symbol grounding problem. *Physica D: Nonlinear Phenomena, 42*, 335–346.

Hutchinson, S., & Louwerse, M. M. (in press). Language statistics explain the spatial-numerical association of response codes. *Psychonomic Bulletin & Review.*

King, L. (2013). *The importance of situational information for abstract concepts.* Dissertation, University of Western Ontario.

Kousta, S., Vigliocco, G., Vinson, D.P., Andrews, M. (2009). Happiness is an abstract word. The role of affect in abstract knowledge representation. In N. Taatgen & H. van Rijn (Eds.). *Proceedings of the 31st Annual Conference of the Cognitive Science Society.* Amsterdam: Cognitive Science Society.

Kousta, S. T., Vigliocco, G., Vinson, D., Andrews, M., & Del Campo, E. (2011). The representation of abstract words: Why emotion matters. *Journal of Experimental Psychology: General, 140,* 14–34. doi:10.1037/a0021446

Kranjec, A., & Chatterjee, A. (2010). Are temporal concepts embodied? A challenge for cognitive neuroscience. *Frontiers in Psychology, 1,* 240. doi:10.3389/fpsyg.2010.00240

Lakoff, G. (1987). *Women, fire, and dangerous things: What categories reveal about the mind.* Chicago: University of Chicago Press.

Lakoff, G., & Johnson, M. (1980). *Metaphors we live by Chicago.* Chicago: Chicago University Press.

Landauer, T., & Dumais, S. (1997). A solutions to Plato's problem: The latent semantic analysis theory of acquisition, induction and representation of knowledge. *Psychological Review, 104,* 211–240.

Louwerse, M. (2008). Embodied relations are encoded in language. *Psychonomic Bulletin & Review, 15,* 838–844.

Louwerse, M. M. (2011). Symbol interdependency in symbolic and embodied cognition. *Topics in Cognitive Science, 3*(2), 273–302.

Louwerse, M. M., & Connell, L. (2011). A taste of words: Linguistic context and perceptual simulation predict the modality of words. *Cognitive Science, 35,* 381–398.

Louwerse, M. M., & Jeuniaux, P. (2008). Language comprehension is both embodied and symbolic. In A. C. G. M. de Vega & A. Glenberg (Eds.), *Symbols and embodiment: Debates on meaning and cognition* (pp. 309–326). Oxford: Oxford University Press.

Louwerse, M. M., & Jeuniaux, P. (2010). The linguistic and embodied nature of conceptual processing. *Cognition, 114*(1), 96–104.

Lugli, L., Baroni, G., Anelli, F., Borghi, A. M., & Nicoletti, R. (2013). Counting is easier while experiencing a congruent motion. *PLoS ONE, 8*(5), e64500. doi:10.1371/journal.pone.0064500

Lugli, L., Baroni, G., Gianelli, C., Borghi, A. M., & Nicoletti, R. (2012). Self, others, objects: How this triadic interaction modulates our behavior. *Memory and Cognition, 40,* 1373–1386.

Madden, C. & Pecher, D. (2010). The force behind language: Are concrete and abstract sentences understood in terms of underlying force patterns? (Manuscript submitted for publication, reported in Pecher et al., 2011).

Mahon, B. Z., & Caramazza, A. (2008). A critical look at the embodied cognition hypothesis and a new proposal for grounding conceptual content. *Journal of Physiology Paris, 102,* 59–70.

Meier, B. P., Hauser, D. J., Robinson, M. D., Friesen, C. K., & Schjeldahl, K. (2007). What's "up" with god? Vertical space as a representation of the divine. *Journal of Personality and Social Psychology, 93,* 699–710.

Meier, B. P., & Robinson, M. D. (2004). Why the sunny side is up: Associations between affect and vertical position. *Psychological Science, 15,* 243–247.

Mirolli, M., & Parisi, D. (2009). Language as a cognitive tool. *Minds and Machines, 19*(4), 517–528.

Murphy, G. L. (1996). On metaphoric representation. *Cognition, 60,* 173–204.

Paivio, A. (1971). *Imagery and verbal processes.* New York: Holt, Rinehart and Winston.

Paivio, A. (1986). *Mental representations: A dual coding approach.* New York: Oxford University.

Paivio, A. (2013). Dual coding theory, word abstractness, and emotion: a critical review of Kousta et al. (2011). *Journal of Experimental Psychology: General, 142*(1):282–287. doi: 10.1037/a0027004

Parkinson, C., & Wheatley, T. (2013). Old cortex, new contexts: Re-purposing spatial perception for social cognition. *Frontiers in Human Neuroscience, 7*, 645. doi:10.3389/fnhum.2013.00645

Pecher, D., Boot, I., & van Dantzig, S. (2011). Abstract concepts: Sensory-motor grounding, metaphors, and beyond. In B. Ross (Ed.), *The psychology of learning and motivation* (Vol. 54, pp. 217–248). Burlington: Academic Press.

Pecher, D., Zeelenberg, R., & Barsalou, L. W. (2003). Verifying different-modality properties for concepts produces switching costs. *Psychological Science, 14*, 119–124.

Pezzulo, G., & Castelfranchi, C. (2007). The symbol detachment problem. *Cognitive Processing, 8*, 115–131.

Prinz, J. J. (2002). *Furnishing the mind: Concepts and their perceptual basis*. Cambridge: MIT Press.

Prinz, J. J. (2005). The return of concept empiricism. In H. Cohen & C. Leferbvre (Eds.), *Categorization and cognitive science*. New Jersey: Elsevier.

Prinz, J. J. (2012). *Beyond human nature. How culture and experience shape our lives.* London: Penguin, New York: Norton.

Prinz, W. (2013). Action representation: Crosstalk between semantics and pragmatics. *Neuropsychologia*. doi: 10.1016/j.neuropsychologia.2013.08.015 (pii: S0028-3932(13)00279-0).

Puglisi, A., Baronchelli, A., & Loreto, V. (2008). Cultural route to the emergence of linguistic categories. *Proceedings of the National Academy of Science, 105*, 7936–7940.

Pulvermüller, F., Shtyrov, Y., & Ilmoniemi, R. (2005). Brain signatures of meaning access in action word recognition. *Journal of Cognitive Neuroscience, 17*, 884–892.

Rizzolatti, G., Camarda, R., Fogassi, L., Gentilucci, M., Luppino, G., & Matelli, M. (1988). Functional organization of inferior area 6 in the macaque monkey. II. Area F5 and the control of distal movements. *Experimental Brain Research, 71*(3), 491–507.

Rizzolatti, G., & Craighero, L. (2004). The mirror neuron system. *Annual Review of Neuroscience, 27*, 169–192.

Roversi, C., Borghi, A. M., & Tummolini, L. (2013). A marriage is an artefact and not a walk that we take together: An experimental study on the categorization of artefacts. *Review of Philosophy and Psychology, 4*(3), 527–542.

Sakreida, K., Scorolli, C., Menz, M.M., Heim, S., Borghi, A.M., Binkofski, F. (2013). Are abstract action words embodied? An fMRI investigation at the interface between language and motor cognition. *Frontiers in Human Neuroscience, 7*, 125.

Schwanenflugel, P. J., Harnishfeger, K. K., & Stowe, R. W. (1988). Context availability and lexical decisions for abstract and concrete words. *Journal of Memory and Language, 27*, 499–520. doi:10.1016/0749-596X(88)90022-8

Scorolli, C., Binkofski, F., Buccino, G., Nicoletti, R., Riggio, L., Borghi, A.M. (2011). Abstract and concrete sentences, embodiment, and languages. *Frontiers in Psychology, 2*, 227. doi: 10.3389/fpsyg.2011.00227.

Scorolli, C., Jacquet, P., Binkofski, F., Nicoletti, R., Tessari, A., Borghi, A.M. (2012). Abstract and concrete phrases processing differently modulates cortico-spinal excitability. *Brain Research, 1488*, 60–71. doi: 10.1016/j.brainres.2012.10.004.

Simmons, W. K., Hamann, S. B., Harenski, C. L., Hu, X. P., & Barsalou, L. W. (2008). fMRI evidence for word association and situated simulation in conceptual processing. *Journal of Physiology Paris, 102*(1–3), 106–119.

Slepian, M. L., & Ambady, N. (2014). Simulating sensorimotor metaphors: Novel metaphors influence sensory judgments. *Cognition, 130*(3), 309–314.

Stanfield, R. A., & Zwaan, R. A. (2001). The effect of implied orientation derived from verbal context on picture recognition. *Psychological Science, 12*, 153–156.

Talmy, L. (1988). Force dynamics in language and cognition. *Cognitive Science, 12*, 49–100.

Tulving, E., & Thomson, D. M. (1973). Encoding specificity and retrieval processes in episodic memory. *Psychological Review, 80*, 352–373.

Van Dantzig, S., Pecher, D., & Zwaan, R. A. (2008). Approach and avoidance as action effect. *Quarterly Journal of Experimental Psychology, 61*, 1298–1306.

Vigliocco, G., Kousta, S. T., Della Rosa, P. A., Vinson, D. P., Tettamanti, M., Devlin, J. T., & Cappa, S. F. (2013a). The neural representation of abstract words: The role of emotion. *Cerebral Cortex.*

Vigliocco, G., Kousta, S., Vinson, D., Andrews, M., & Del Campo, E. (2013b).The representation of abstract words: What matters? Reply to Paivio's (2013) comment on Kousta et al. (2011). *Journal of Experimental Psychology: General, 142*(1):288–291. doi: 10.1037/a0028749

Wiemer-Hastings, K., & Xu, X. (2005). Content differences for abstract and concrete concepts. *Cognitive Science, 29*, 719–736.

Wilson-Mendenhall, C. D., Simmons, W. K., Martin, A., & Barsalou, L. W. (2014). Contextual processing of abstract concepts reveals neural representations of non-linguistic semantic content. *Journal of Cognitive Neuroscience, 25*(6), 920–935.

Winner, E., Rosenstiel, A. K., & Gardner, H. (1976). The development of metaphoric understanding. *Developmental Psychology, 12*(4), 289–297.

Zwaan, R. A., & Yaxley, R. H. (2003). Spatial iconicity affects semantic relatedness judgment. *Psychonomic Bulletin & Review, 10*(4), 954–958.

Chapter 4
Word Learning and Word Acquisition

I have always tried to write in a simple way, using down-to-earth and not abstract words.

Georges Simenon

4.1 Introduction

In the previous chapters, we have proposed that the difference in representation between concrete and abstract words might be due to their different acquisition modality. The aim of this chapter is to explore the rich literature on word learning and word acquisition and to illustrate evidence on how these processes occur that might be relevant for the WAT proposal. First, we will outline approaches that emphasize the importance of social aspects in word learning, and then, we will turn to embodied approaches highlighting the role of perception and action in word acquisition. We will also show that some hybrid approaches have been proposed, in which both social-linguistic and perception–action elements are taken into account. According to them, multiple and different cues might lead to word learning, and the role of perception and action cues might have more weight in the early phases of word learning, while the role of social and linguistic cues might be more prominent once children master some social abilities and possess a consistent vocabulary. We will then describe the literature on modality of acquisition, according to which different kinds of words, concrete and abstract, might be learned through different strategies. Finally, we will report some acquisition studies with adults realized in our laboratory. In this review, we have no pretense of being exhaustive in providing an overall framework of studies on children word acquisition. We simply intend to outline approaches and illustrate evidence that are in line with and that provide support to the WAT proposal.

4.2 Social Aspects in Word Learning

Research on conceptual development has been widely influenced by the image of the child as a lonely learner, advancing and testing hypotheses on his/her own, as shown by Gelman (2009) in her critical review. In contrast with this view of

A. M. Borghi and F. Binkofski, *Words as Social Tools: An Embodied View on Abstract Concepts*, SpringerBriefs in Cognition,
DOI: 10.1007/978-1-4614-9539-0_4, © The Author(s) 2014

children as lonely hypotheses testers, every form of learning, even if apparently self-directed, relies on a social and cultural milieu, which is often taken for granted, and therefore not investigated. We will briefly overview some research lines where the importance of social input for children's word learning has been highlighted. First, we will illustrate studies that put some emphasis on the social aspects involved in language learning, as the approaches of Vygotsky, of cultural psychology, and of comparative studies, for example, by Tomasello and collaborators. Then, we will turn to studies that show that children—and adults as well—use different modalities to acquire words, one more based on perception, one more linguistic and other combinations of the two aforementioned ones. Finally, we will describe studies on testimony that demonstrate the kind of linguistic contribution adults give to children's learning.

4.2.1 Cultural Psychology and Vygotsky

An obvious exception to the individualistic way of conceiving children's learning is given by cultural psychology, an area of psychology that considers mind and culture as strictly interwoven and which focuses on the impact of culture on human thought, questioning universalist's assumptions on the human mind (e.g., Bruner 1990; Nisbett 2003; Nisbett et al. 2001; Shweder 1991). In this area, demonstrations are flourishing, showing that experimental results obtained in Western industrialized societies cannot be generalized and considered as universal (e.g., Henrich et al. 2010; Medin and Atran 2004; see also Prinz 2012); rather, culture has a marked impact on cognition.

This view relies heavily on the thought of the well-known Russian psychologist Vygotsky (1978, 1981, 1986, 1987). The distinction proposed by Vygotsky between scientific and spontaneous concepts is relevant and fully in line with the WAT proposal, since it partly mirrors the distinction between concrete and abstract concepts we proposed. Let us briefly analyze Vygostky's thought on this topic (see Karpov and Bransford 2005). Compared to spontaneous, everyday concepts, scientific concepts are more general and have a systematic organization and are related primarily to other concepts rather than to the object or event they refer to. "The interdependence between spontaneous and scientific concepts stems from the special relations existing between the scientific concept and the object. In the scientific concepts that the child acquires in school, the relation to an object is mediated from the start by some other concept. Thus, the very notion of scientific concept implies a certain position in relation to other concepts, i.e., a place within a system of concepts." (Vygotsky 1986, p. 172).

Crucially to us, the acquisition of scientific concepts differs from that of everyday spontaneous concepts. Spontaneous concepts are learned through the guidance of adults but during children's everyday activities, such as play and interaction with others; for this reason, they are not systematic and for a while they remain unconscious. The acquisition of both kinds of concepts is thus guided by a social input, but while spontaneous concepts are learned participating in the activities in which they are typically used, learning of scientific concepts typically occurs in a specialized setting and requires systematic forms of instruction. "The development of the scientific… concept, a phenomenon that occurs as part of the educational process, constitutes a unique form of systematic cooperation between the teacher and the child. The maturation of the child's higher mental functions occurs in this cooperative process, that is, it occurs through the adult's assistance and participation. In the domain of interest to us, this is expressed in the growth of the relativeness of causal thinking and in the development of a certain degree of voluntary control in scientific thinking. This element of voluntary control is a product of the instructional process itself." (DSC, pp. 168, 169, original emphases).

The systematic forms of instruction required to learn scientific concepts imply the use of verbal definitions. Learning of scientific concepts differs from learning of everyday concepts also because of this explicit linguistic mediation.

> The child becomes conscious of his spontaneous concepts relatively late; the ability to define them in words, to operate with them at will, appears long after he has acquired the concepts. He has the concept (i.e., knows the object to which the concept refers), but is not conscious of his own act of thought. The development of a scientific concept, on the other hand, usually begins with its verbal definition and its use in non-spontaneous operations—with working on the concept itself. It starts its life in the child's mind at the level that his spontaneous concepts reach only later. (Vygotsky, p. 192).

4.2.2 Studies on Testimony

Studies on "testimony" are highly relevant for the WAT theory, as they qualify the role adults play in shaping children's knowledge. Two different views on testimony are present in the literature. According to the first, children trust only testimony that extends the empirical data they can collect on their own, without contradicting their own observations. However, recent evidence has revealed that children rely on testimony not only in domains such as psychology, cosmology, and biology, where testimony can extend their observations, but in domains such as theology as well, for example, when they receive information about God and the afterlife. Indeed, in some cases, explanations are the only possible source of information for acquiring some concepts, such as scientific concepts, supernatural concepts (e.g., "God"), concepts for which there is no correspondence between the perceptual features and the scientific classifications (e.g., "bats," "whales"), and social concepts (e.g., "race," "ethnicity," etc.). Let us leave aside concepts for which there is no correspondence between the scientific classification and the perceptual basis. Apart from those, which might have a concrete referent, all other concepts are subsets of what we consider the general category of abstract concepts.

Harris and Koenig (2006) review evidence showing how children acquire key concepts that they cannot observe first-hand and verify empirically, relying on others' testimony: There is evidence that they acquire through testimony knowledge on the relationship between the brain and the mental processes, on the spheric shape of the earth (Vosniadou 1994), on the life-cycle and the relationship between the death and the possession of vital internal organs (Jaakkola and Slaughter 2002). More crucially, children form abstract notion of domains where they do not have direct experience. For example, they form the abstract notion of God, progressively acknowledging that he has extraordinary cognitive, biological, and creative powers; importantly, their view is not autonomously developed but is heavily influenced by the beliefs of the community of which they are part, since the differences between fundamentalist and non-fundamentalist communities are marked. This suggests that children do not invent these powers, but rather rely on the knowledge of their community members. The same is true for the notion of afterlife. Even if children rely on testimony of others, they are not passively receptors of the information they gather. In all cases, children actively rework the information they receive and integrate it with their previous knowledge. The same can be true for ideology, even if we are not aware of literature specifically investigating the influences of ideology on children's thought.

One interesting example of this active search for information is the questions children ask adults, for example, the persistent "why" questions between 3 and 6 years. While these questions often concern anomalies children register during their interaction with the world (e.g., "Why doesn't butter stay on top of hot toast?" "How is it that when we put our hand into the water, we don't make a hole in it?"), in some cases, they pertain spiritual domains, i.e., domains of which they cannot have direct experience. In some cases, they pose a persistent series of questions, engaging in what have been called real "passages of intellectual search" (Tizard and Hughes 1984). Crucial to us is the fact that when they register an anomaly, they refer to adults to ask for conciliatory clarifications and explanations. Importantly, they seem to trust adults as reliable sources of information to understand hidden and mechanistic causes of events, in a variety of domains.

The credibility of adults is carefully evaluated. Sabbagh and Baldwin (2001) demonstrated that 3- and 4-year-olds are sensitive to explicit cues given by informants: Children prefer to learn new words from people who declare knowledge rather than ignorance, and from people who declare certainty rather than from people who are uncertain and use locutions as "mmm, maybe," etc. These studies reveal that during word learning, children do not pay attention only to the relationship between a word and its referent, but also to the characteristics of the speaker who teaches a word: No word learning occurs when the speaker reveals uncertainty, even if there is no referential ambiguity.

Other studies reveal that children are sensitive also to less explicit cues and are able to take into account the accuracy of others. Trust in adults is influenced by familiarity with them but can be revoked: in a study with children aged 3–5 years, Corriveau and Harris (2009) demonstrated that children preferred to trust familiar over unfamiliar teachers who named novel objects and pantomimed their function. However, they were also able to monitor the accuracy of their informants: While for younger children, the trust in their familiar informants was not affected by inaccurate information, 4- and particularly 5-year-old children took accuracy into account: On this basis, if familiar teachers were not accurate, they tended to revoke their trust in them. Further studies reveal that children's learning is modulated by the trust in the people from whom they are learning, in a variety of domains and not only during language learning. 3- and 4-year-olds keep in mind specific information on other people's accuracy and spontaneously use it during learning: For example, when they have to choose between conflicting information in learning to use a tool, they rely on the cues given by the informant who has demonstrated to be more accurate in the past (Birch et al. 2008).

Overall, literature on testimony is important for the WAT view: It shows that children are prone to receiving information and clarifications by adults, that they accurately monitor the accuracy of the information they receive, and it reveals that the ability to learn language and to learn overall is strictly interwoven with children's social abilities. At the same time, literature on testimony shows that the information provided by others is particularly precious in domains where the perceptual inputs are insufficient or lacking, as the domains that pertain abstract concepts and words.

4.2.3 Comparative Studies on Apes and Children

The role of social imitation and of socio-pragmatic aspects in human word learning has been stressed by comparative studies that highlighted the role social learning plays for our species. One of the main contributions of this literature can be summarized with the following words by Tomasello and Akhtar (2000): "Although learning object labels may appear to involve straightforward mapping of word to referent…, it also requires the social-cognitive ability to tune into speakers' referential intention" (p. 130).

According to the socio-pragmatic theory of language acquisition (e.g., Tomasello 1992), language acquisition is an intrinsically social phenomenon. An important building block of the capability to acquire language is given by the culturally inherited ability to imitate others—our species is endowed with the capability to imitate, while other social species only emulate actions. The capability to learn language is possible only when entering into a joint attention based activity with adults language speakers (Bruner 1983; Tomasello 1992).

Importantly, word learning is not limited to the association between an auditory input and the referent. Rather, the role of intersubjective aspects is crucial for language acquisition. In order to learn language children engage in joint activities with adults, they benefit from a variety of cues, not only from linguistic cues. For example, a very important social cue to determine reference is gaze direction. Children rely on the gaze direction of adults when they pronounce new words in the presence of multiple objects; they rely on others' gaze even if the adult is looking into a bucket and the target object is invisible to the children (Baldwin 1993). Already 24-month-old children rely on adults' gaze direction rather than on objects perceptual salience (Tomasello and Akhtar 2000).

Overall, research has shown that linguistic cues are relevant but not the only information source at the basis of language learning. According to a more classic approach, children rely on constraints to learn new words (Markman 1989; Nelson 1988). For example, they assume that two different words apply to different objects and have difficulties in applying the same word to the same referent (e.g., "animal," "dog," "Fufi") (mutual exclusivity constraint); in addition, in the absence of counter-indications, they assume that a novel word refers to an object (whole object constraint). The approach based on constraints is founded on the assumption that it might be difficult to determine reference only on the basis of pragmatic cues, since they might be ambiguous.

In contrast, a number of studies and researches favouring the socio-pragmatic view have emphasized the richness of the pragmatic and social context (Tomasello and Akhtar 1995). Children take into account the whole pragmatic and discourse context and are sensitive to a variety of social cues: They register the activities of adults, what they are doing and why, they are able to detect their intention to act and to predict the outcome of their actions, they are able to determine what is new for them; more generally, they benefit from a variety of information that goes well beyond the linguistic inputs. Gergely et al. (1995) have demonstrated with beautifully designed experiments that one-year-old infants are able to interpret and predict others' goal-directed actions and that they possess a theory of rational action. Tomasello et al. (2005) have shown that the human specificity cannot be limited to the capability to understand others' intentions. Other species are also able to understand the intentions of others, but they do not engage in social and cultural activities with others. 6-month-olds perceive others and follow their gaze, being able to predict the outcome of familiar actions; at 9-month babies are able to understand that people have goals and persist in order to accomplish them, at 14, they are able to understand intentional actions. On this basis, they can start forms of imitative learning, in which they make an action plan to pursue a given goal. In spite of the importance of intention understanding, according to Tomasello et al. (2005) what is specifically and uniquely human is the so-called "shared intentionality," the ability to create joint actions and to be involved in collaborative activities with others. Apes have a sophisticated capability of understanding the intentions of others, but they lack the motivation and ability in exchanging emotions and experiences and in engaging in common activities as humans do. Instead, children from 9 to 12 months engage in a series of triadic behaviors, involving the child, an adult and an object—a variety of joint attentional skills emerge, as for example, following the gaze direction of the other, pointing to an object, holding it to show it to someone, imitating the gestures of others with the object. Language learning is grounded in these abilities (Tomasello 2000). In this perspective, language is a prominent outer sign of this intrinsically social character of human cognition: "What is language if not a set of coordination devices for directing the attention of others?" (Tomasello et al. 2005, p. 16). Importantly for us, according to Tomasello (2000) the basic linguistic units are not single words, but utterances and the first utterances children produce are concrete ones, i.e., instantiations of item-based schemas, while later abstraction emerges from generalizing across a variety of different schemas.

Overall, the studies that compare apes and children cognition and language learning are highly relevant for the WAT proposal. They stress indeed the importance of the social aspects for human learning, and they ground language learning in social abilities, in particular in joint attention and shared intentionality capabilities. Furthermore, they testify that children learn within a context, heavily relying on adults' collaboration, that learning concerns utterances rather than words, and that the acquisition process goes from concrete instantiations to more abstract constructions.

4.3 Embodiment and Statistics in Word Learning

A different way out to the problem posed by constraints is provided by the empiricist approach to word learning. As previously outlined, a more traditional approach is based on the idea that children use constraints to guide their word learning process. In fact, given the richness of the perceptual input, a problem of referential ambiguity is present: A heard word can be referred to single objects, to their parts, or to different aspects in a scene. To solve this referential ambiguity, children need constraints: for example, they assume that each object is referred to by a single word (Markman 1989). Recent work by Smith and collaborators (Yu and Smith 2007; Smith and Yu 2008) shows that 12- to 14-month-old children and adults solve the referential problem not by relying on constraints, but rather by computing statistics across trials. For example, the word "ball" is experienced across different scenes, in which not only a ball but different items are present. Children have the impressive ability to keep track of the different word occurrences, in order to solve the problem of the referent of the word "ball," and later they become able to attach the label to the proper referent. A higher number of words and of referents provides clearer evidence, thus it leads to a better learning: Yu and Smith (2007) demonstrated that adults learned more word-referent pairs with sets containing 18 words and referents than with sets with only nine words and referents. The role of cross-situational learning, according to which multiple meanings are encoded across different situations using statistical procedures, is not uncontroversial and is challenged by evidence that indicate that learners use instead a one-trial fast mapping procedure, hypothesizing a single meaning and maintaining this hypothesis across different trials (see Medina et al. 2011). Despite this, experiments and models that show how statistical learning can account for word-to-referent mappings are growing. According to this empiricist account, words are learned by mapping them with their referents, through an associative process. For example, Smith (2005) spoke of a dumb attentional mechanism which characterizes word learning, leading to the associations of words with perceptually salient inputs. A particularly salient perceptual property is shape, probably due to the fact that it is not only a visual but also an action-based property (Smith 2005).

Shape is indeed a truly embodied object property. An impressive number of experiments starting from the seminal paper by Landau et al. (1988) have shown that children of the Western societies extend nouns on the basis of similarity in shape. When taught a new name (e.g., when they are told "This is a dax"), children extend it to objects similar in shape rather than in color, texture, or other perceptual properties. The shape bias becomes rather stable at around 2 years. Importantly, however, infants are not passive recipients of information, and perceptual inputs are not passively experienced. Infants actively move in the environment, search for objects, and focus their attention on some of them. Intriguing new data obtained tracking infants' gaze with head-mounted cameras indicate that infants learn new names focusing attention on an object within a scene. In this way, they maximize the role played by co-occurrence statistics. In a clever study, 15-month-olds were presented with two objects and two names for each trial. The looking pattern of infants who were able to learn the new names suggests that statistical learning is important for learning, but further mechanisms are necessary to maximize the information it gives. One important mechanism is embodied selective attention: Statistical learning succeeds if infants are able to focus on the named object, "cleaning" the perceptual input when it is too complex. Gaze direction, head movements, and hand movements (for example, holding the object) contribute in reducing the ambiguity of the input. Yu and Smith (2012) used head-mounted cameras for infants and parents and found that infants actively move to select an object, making the eyes and the head closer to it and holding it in the hands. In this way, they focus on it reducing the role of potential distractors. Parents typically, but not always, provided the names in optimal sensory moments, when the object was under the infant's attentional focus; when they chose the optimal sensory moment, word learning occurred. Data of this kind provide a clear indication of how infants' movements and actions, together with social stimuli, contribute in selecting attention on the object to be named and create the optimal conditions for statistical learning to occur. Importantly, recent evidence (e.g., Wojcik and Saffran 2013) reveals that during word learning, children do not only learn mappings between a word and a referent, but encode also information on the relations between objects, as for example, the similarities among word referents. 2-year-olds were taught four novel words referring to four novel objects, grouped in two pairs of visually similar objects. Then, they listened to the repetition of word pairs: Results showed that they listened longer to word pairs referring to similar than to dissimilar objects.

Further literature is in keeping with the idea that the kind of input given has a strong impact on language acquisition and later on language mastering, as revealed, for example, in reading and comprehension abilities. Here, we do not intend to enter into the nature-nurture debate, discussing whether language acquisition is innately pre-specified or whether learning plays a major role, since this is outside the aims of this book. Notice, however, that stressing the role played by the kind of input is in line with the general idea that language is learned rather than innately pre-specified, as studies focusing on language statistical learning in infants and children are beginning to demonstrate (e.g., Saffran et al. 1996;

Romberg and Saffran 2010; Gomez and Gerken 1999, 2000). Research on statistical learning has shown that infants develop remarkable abilities in parsing language into word-like constituents based on combinations of syllables, in encoding word order information, in abstracting over linguistic categories as determiners, adjectives, verbs, and nouns. Importantly, it has been shown that experience with statistical cues that mark categorical distinctions provides the basis for learning word meanings (e.g., Lany and Saffran 2010). In addition, recent results have pointed out that the ability to attend to and to keep track of statistical regularities in matching words and referent is at the basis of the word learning capability (Smith and Yu 2008; Yu and Smith 2007). Overall, this line of research questions the centrality of semantics for word acquisition, revealing that the development of semantic and syntactic competence might be more intertwined than previously thought.

Overall, studies show that word learning occurs through the associations between words and referents, which investigate the mechanisms of statistical learning, and that reveal how embodied selective attention contributes to focus attention on single objects and to learn their name are highly relevant to the WAT proposal. They stress indeed the fact that word learning is an embodied and grounded process.

4.4 Hybrid Approaches of Word Learning

As we have seen, both social and perception–action aspects contribute to word learning. Some recent views propose that both perceptual and social aspects count, but that they might have a different weight at different ages. Evidence supports this view suggesting that very young children are more sensitive to perceptual aspects, becoming progressively interested in social cues when contrasted with perceptual salience. Pruden et al. (2006) investigated how 10-month-old babies learn novel words, trying to disentangle the perceptual and the social dimensions. Babies were shown interesting objects, i.e., brightly colored objects either producing sounds or with moving parts, and boring objects, i.e., objects gray and uniform in color that did not produce sounds nor had moving parts. An experimenter taught them a new label for the objects (e.g., "MODI"). In the coincidental condition, the name was referred to the perceptually interesting object, in the conflict condition to the boring one. In the new label test trial, they were taught a new name for the object (e.g., "look at the GLORP, not at the MODI"), the hypothesis being that if they had already learned a name for the object, they should look away from it, due to the mutual exclusivity constraint. In the final recovery task, they were told to look at the "MODI" again. Visual fixation times were analyzed, and the pattern of results was straightforward: In the recovery test, the babies attached the label to the perceptually salient object, not to the socially interesting one. The objection that no word learning occurred, and that children simply looked at the most interesting object, was ruled out by the results of the new label test: As predicted, children looked away from the object to find a novel object to name. At 12 months, the pattern is already different, since children seem to be sensitive to social cues: They learn a new label for a novel object when the social and the perceptual cues are aligned; otherwise, no evidence of word learning is present. Thus, children are responsive to social cues, but they do not recruit them for word learning. At 19 and 24 months, the social cues dominate: learning of new words occurred for socially interesting objects, independently of whether they were perceptually interesting or boring. On the basis of this kind of data, the hybrid emergentist coalition model (ECM) has been proposed (Hollich et al. 2000; Hirsh-Pasek et al. 2000, 2004; Golinkoff and Hirsh-Pasek 2006). According to ECM, multiple cues are at the basis of word acquisition, and different processes characterize the early and the later stages of word learning: "As they break through the language barrier, children are guided (though not completely) by associationist laws. As they mature into veteran word learners, they are guided (though not completely) by socio-pragmatic strategies." (Hirsh-Pasek et al. 2004). To test the model, a variety of experiments were run on three different samples: 12- to 13-month-olds who are starting to learn words; 19- to 20-month-olds who may or may not have yet experienced a vocabulary spurt; and 24- to 25-month-olds who typically master a large production vocabulary. They tested reference and found that children initially rely on perceptual similarity and then become progressively more sensitive to social cues; furthermore, they tested extendibility, i.e., they investigated whether children adopt a "narrow to large" principle, starting with a proper noun hypothesis, initially adequate for a given object, and analyzed the perceptual and social cues on the basis of which they extended it to other category members. The overall pattern of results suggests that children use multiple cues for word learning and that depending on their maturity level, they are able to appreciate their variety: Initially, they rely on perceptual cues, later they are able to appreciate the role played by social ones. This developmental trend would also help clarify why early word learning is rather slow (1–2 words per week) compared to faster word learning occurring after 19 months of age. Support to this, view comes also from further studies. For example, Weizman and Snow (2001) investigated mother–child conversations in 5 settings (e.g., play, mealtime, and book readings). 99 % of maternal lexical input consisted of the 3,000 most frequent words. They found that early exposure to sophisticated linguistic input, i.e., to words beyond the 3,000 most common in English, had a marked influence on children's later vocabulary performance, more than the quantity of lexical input overall. Woodward et al. (1994) studying word learning in 13- and 18-month-old children, speculated, "Perhaps prenaming explosion children have highly effective nonlinguistic associative mechanisms that allow them to map sound patterns onto the environmental entities that are presented with them, whereas postnaming explosion children learn words through more advanced linguistic mechanisms" (p. 564).

Hybrid models, according to which more cues—perceptual and social—coexist to promote word learning, are highly relevant to the WAT proposal. However, in the WAT theory, we do not focus on age differences, but on differences in kind of words. Even more in line with the WAT view are proposals according to which perceptual and linguistic information contribute differently to learning of different kinds of words, as evidence on modality of acquisition we will review in the Chap. 6 will help to clarify. These proposals start from the consideration that words refer to the world in multiple ways and that not all are equally easy to learn. Gentner (2006) proposes that children learn first words the referents of which can be easily individuated, as proper nouns of animate entities and concrete nouns. Other words, such as verbs and abstract words, are learned later. In the same vein, Gleitman et al. (2005) distinguish between hard words, more abstract and therefore more difficult to acquire, and easy words. They move from the consideration that early learning seems to be predicted by the "concreteness" of words, rather than by a specific word class: for example, children learn the verb "kiss" before the noun "idea" and even before the noun "kiss," while they acquire the verbs "think" and "know" later than the verbs "hit" and "go." At the same time, they claim that the very concept of "concreteness" is vague and needs to be sharpened. Gleitman et al. (2005) overview a series of studies they performed, reported in Gillette et al. (1999), and Snedeker and Gleitman (2004), aimed at studying learning of easy and hard words. In these studies, they used the human simulation paradigm (HSP): They had adults observe short video-clips of mother–child interactions recorded in natural situations. In some experiments, video-clips were silenced, and when the mother pronounced a "mystery word," participants heard a beep. The same word was presented in six video-clips in sequence. Later participants had to guess which was the "mystery word." Their performance differed consistently depending on the word and reflected the order of acquisition of words in children. Concrete nouns referring to whole objects/entities ("elephant") were easier to identify than abstract nouns ("idea"), and concrete verbs ("throw") were identified faster than abstract ones ("know"). In further experiments, participants had to perform the same task, but they received different sources of information as a cue: They were either given visual information, i.e., the video-clips, or linguistic content information, consisting in further names occurring in the mother's utterances, or linguistic syntactic information, in which the frames in which the word occurred were presented, but where the content words and the mystery words were substituted by nonsense words (e.g., "Why don't ver GORP telfa?"). The visual cues were most useful for nouns and concrete terms, while for abstract terms, syntactic information was critical: for example, visual cues were useful to identify "go" but not "know," while the opposite was true for syntactic cues. On the basis of evidence of this kind, Gleitman et al. (2005) propose that the first words, which typically are basic level concrete nouns, are rather easily acquired through a word-to-world mapping mechanism. In contrast, there exist words which are more difficult to acquire, the "hard words," which are typically more abstract. Once provided with a substantial amount of easy words, children—but also adults, during word acquisition—can proceed to the process of structure-to-world mapping. In order to acquire abstract words, a consistent amount of sophisticated linguistic knowledge is necessary. Syntactic information contributes to this acquisition process, so that syntax and semantics should be considered as deeply intertwined: Word meaning can be learned probabilistically, and hard words can be learned with the help of other linguistic information.

Basically, word learning occurs probabilistically, and it benefits from different sources, linguistic and extralinguistic. What changes with time is the capability to master linguistic information. Indeed, children hardly master syntax during the acquisition of the first 100 words, which are mostly concrete. Only later, when the amount of learned words triplicates, they demonstrate the capability to use syntax. In this perspective, the later acquisition of abstract words would not be due to the necessity of a conceptual change, but to informational reasons: Many other words should be acquired as they can provide the background for the acquisition of hard words.

4.5 Age of Acquisition and Modality of Acquisition

An important support to the WAT view comes from literature on modality of acquisition (MOA) (Wauters et al. 2003). MOA is a new construct referring to the kind of input children receive while acquiring the meaning of a word or of a sign. The child can acquire a word meaning perceptually, linguistically, or benefiting from both modalities. The most frequent acquisition modality is perceptual: for example, the child experiences different red objects and entities and, in different occasions, he/she consistently hears the word “red”. The same is true for other words having a concrete referent, such as bottle, doll, and house. The situation differs for a word like “century,” and for the majority of the words, we called “abstract”: The child cannot directly experience their referent, thus he/she has to rely on someone else’s explanations or definitions, be they spoken, written, fingerspelled, or signed, or he/she has to infer its meaning from spoken, written, fingerspelled, or signed information. In many cases, both perceptual and linguistic information contribute to word acquisition. MOA does not depend only on the type of concept but also on the type of context: for example, words like “tundra” or “snow” can be acquired perceptually by children living in some areas but have to be acquired linguistically by others. Similarly, children whose parents are carpenter will learn perceptually the meaning of carpentry tool words that other children will learn only through the linguistic mediation. Differently from concreteness and imageability, thus, MOA is context-dependent. MOA can be determined by asking adults to rate words for acquisition modality on a 5-point scale. MOA is correlated with imageability (0.64), concreteness (0.47), and age of acquisition (0.59), but it does not overlap with them. It can help explaining why abstract words are learned later than concrete ones. An analysis of the elementary school textbooks revealed a progressive increase in linguistically provided information over perceptual information. Finally, MOA is influenced by the possibility to access to complete perceptual and linguistic information or not: On this basis, it explains differences in comprehension by children who cannot see or hear. In some experiments, hearing and deaf children between 7 and 15 years of age were required to read sentences in which a target word was present and to answer a question after reading it by pushing a yes or no button; both reading times and comprehension measures were taken (Wauters et al. 2008). Reading times were faster and comprehension scores were higher for perceptually acquired than for linguistically acquired words for both groups; the difference between the two modalities decreased with age only for hearing children. In addition, MOA proved to be an important factor in explaining the poorer reading comprehension of deaf compared to hearing children. Texts with a high proportion of words rated as being learned linguistically are difficult for deaf children.

Overall, studies on MOA are highly relevant to the WAT proposal, for a number of reasons. First, they draw attention to the role played by the input given to children and to the different acquisition modality of words. Second, they point out that words rated as linguistically acquired are more difficult to read and to comprehend compared to perceptually acquired words. Third, they show an increase with age of linguistically acquired words in educational textbooks, probably due to the emphasis put first on decoding and only later on acquiring information. Fourth, they give some hints as to the process of words acquisition in the course of the development: Interesting parallels can be drawn between the later acquisition of words through language and the later acquisition of abstract words, which do not possess a concrete perceivable referent.

4.6 Acquisition of Novel Words in Adults: An Embodied Approach

We will briefly illustrate two studies on novel categories and word acquisition in adults, performed in our lab, the results of which support the WAT view. Both studies were aimed at testing the following general hypotheses:

(a) Linguistic (and social) information should play a major role for the representation of abstract categories and word meanings, while sensorimotor information is more crucial for the representation of concrete ones. We will review only the aspects of the studies that are relevant to the present discussion.
(b) Perception and action information should be crucial for both, but the higher differences within the exemplars of abstract categories and the complex relations that characterize them compared to the greater compactness of concrete categories should render the linguistic input more relevant for the first.
(c) The different acquisition modality of concrete and abstract categories should have an influence not only on the way we represent them, but also on how we respond to them with our body: Abstract categories and words should activate more mouth responses, concrete categories, and words' hand responses. Notice, however, that this would not be true for concrete words the meaning of which explicitly refers to the hand or mouth, as "finger," "tongue," etc. (Bergen et al. 2003; Bergen 2012).

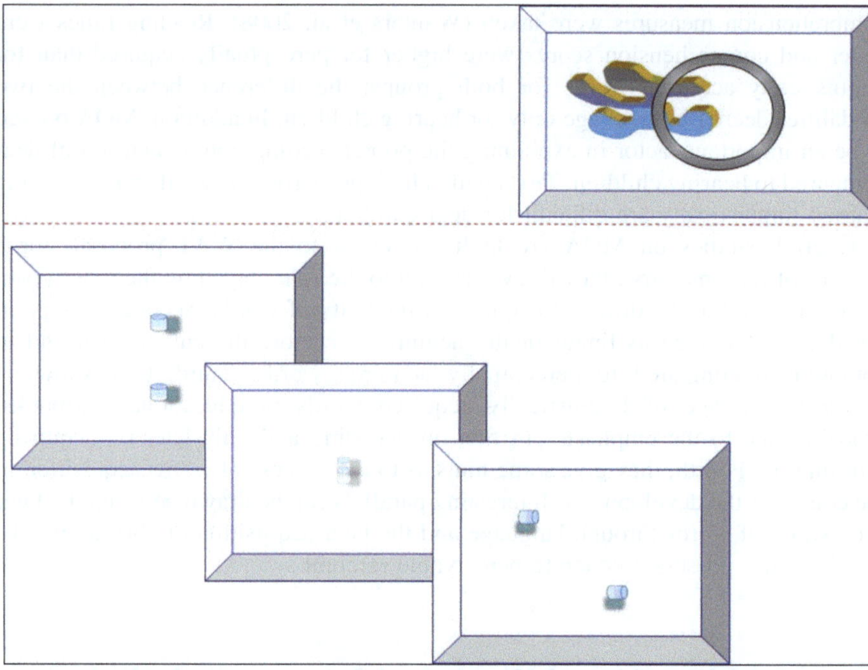

Fig. 4.1 Study by Borghi et al. (2011). Some examples of the stimuli we used. Exemplars of concrete categories consisted of bidimensional novel objects with *bright colors*; participants could manipulate them with the mouse and were required to verify whether they fitted into a *donut shaped* figure. Exemplars of abstract categories were composed by two or more elements of a *bluish uniform color* which moved and interacted in novel ways; participants could simply observe their interactions

Borghi et al. (2011) presented adult participants with novel objects to explore. Concrete objects were bidimensional novel objects with bright colors, abstract concepts were composed by two or more elements of uniform color which moved and interacted in novel ways. Participants had some time to study them: They were allowed to "manipulate" concrete objects, moving them with the mouse on the screen, while they could simply observe the abstract concepts (see Fig. 4.1).

Later, we verified whether participants were able to form a category, asking them whether two objects belonged to the same category or not. Results showed that it was more difficult to form abstract than concrete categories, in line with what happens in real life. Later participants were taught the novel category name—they read on the screen "This is a fusapo/a calona, etc.". In half of the cases, they were also given a written explanation of the category meaning, as for example, "clash between two elements, which later separate." In a further test, they had to answer by pressing a key on a keyboard whether the object they saw had a given name. Again, abstract words showed a disadvantage compared to concrete words (see Fig. 4.2).

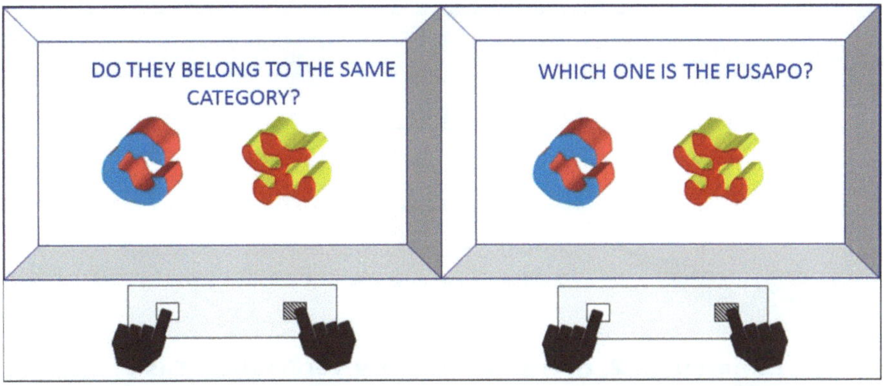

Fig. 4.2 Study by Borghi et al. (2011). An example of two of the tasks we used. The first task, a categorical recognition one, was aimed at verifying the facility to form categories independently from knowing their name. Participants were required to press two different keys on the keyboard to decide whether two objects belonged to the same category or not. In the second task, aimed at verifying the effect of labels on categorization, participants were instructed to press a different key on the keyboard depending on whether the label corresponded to the object they saw or not

When given the names of concrete and abstract categories and asked to produce their properties, participants produced the properties typically found in property generation tasks, respectively, for concrete and abstract concepts, i.e., more perceptual properties for the first and more abstract and general statements for the second. This test gave us the guarantee that the novel concrete and abstract categories we used corresponded in content and structure-to-real-life ones. The most crucial test experiments, however, consisted in a property verification task. Participants had to respond by pressing a key on the keyboard with the hand or by saying "yes" on the microphone if the property was typically true of the category. Response time results showed that abstract words were responded to faster with the microphone, particularly if not only the label but the explanation as well had been given, while responses to concrete words were faster with the keyboard (see Fig. 4.3).

A control experiment showed that the advantage of the microphone over the keyboard with abstract words was not present if they were not grounded, i.e., if the information provided by perceptual input and that provided by the linguistic input (label plus explanation) were dissociated. Even if no data on acquisition were collected, the results of this study suggest that concrete and abstract words might be acquired relying on different cues, perceptual and linguistic. Linguistic cues, i.e., both labels and notably explanations, were more relevant for abstract words. These results thus contribute to foster the idea that different acquisition modalities are present and have a different weight in concrete and abstract words representation. One important aspect of the study is that it reveals that these different acquisition modalities have a direct bodily consequence, as they activate different

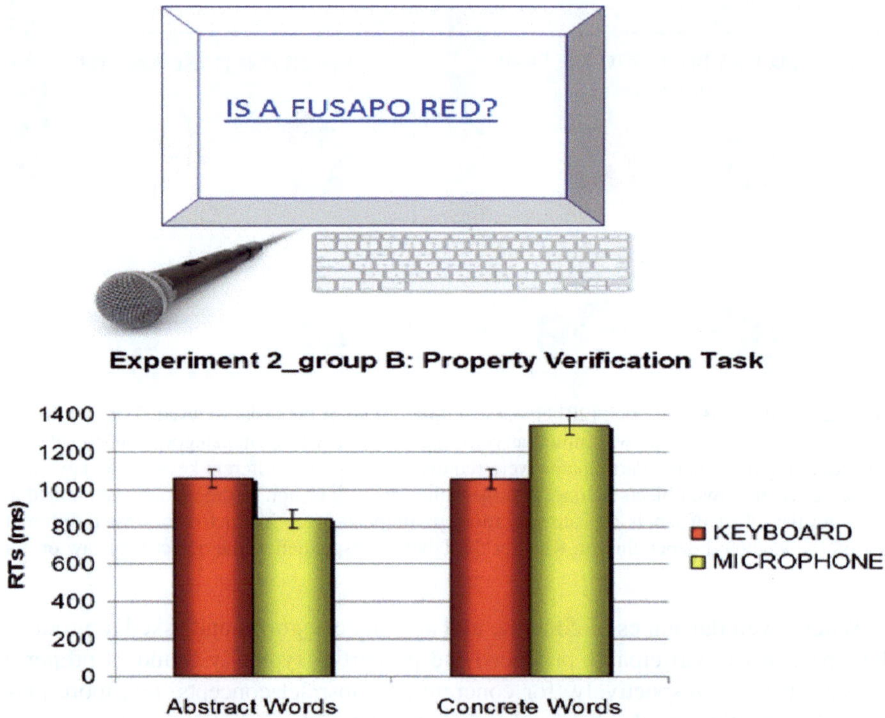

Fig. 4.3 Study by Borghi et al. (2011). The interaction obtained in the property verification task showing that responses to abstract words were faster with the microphone and that responses with the concrete words were faster with the keyboard

parts of our body and of our motor system: Abstract words lead to the activation of the mouth, concrete words to the activation of the hand.

In a recent study, Granito et al. (in preparation) used a similar paradigm, but introduced some variations. In order to train subjects with more ecological materials, instead of using shapes presented on the computer screen, participants were given objects composed by Lego bricks. Exemplars of concrete categories consisted of single objects composed by different parts, while exemplars of abstract categories were composed of the same objects arranged in complex and different relations (see Fig. 4.4).

Thus, while in the previous study, concrete words were defined as referring to single, perceptually varied manipulable objects and abstract words as referring to complex objects moving in different ways, here the focus of the distinction between concrete and abstract concepts lies in their different degree of complexity and in the fact that the latter can be defined as referring to relations rather than to single objects. Both concrete and abstract words' referents are perceivable/ manipulable, but the exemplars of concrete categories were similar from a sensorimotor point of view, those of abstract categories were not. Each relation

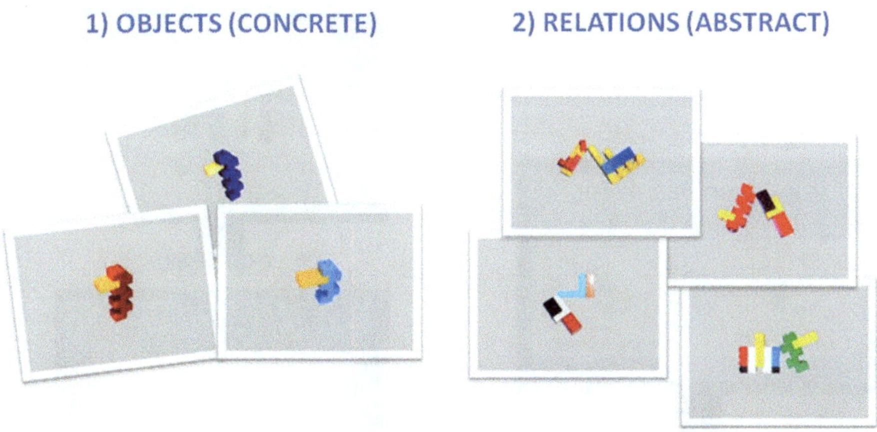

Fig. 4.4 Study by Granito et al. (in preparation). Some examples of stimuli we used, composed by Lego bricks. Exemplars of concrete categories consisted of single objects composed by different parts, while exemplars of abstract categories were composed of the same objects arranged in complex and different relations

category was defined exclusively by the spatial relation existing among the component objects, e.g., "the two objects have two contact points," and the spatial relation remained constant across the category exemplars. As a result, members of concrete categories were similar from a sensorimotor point of view, while members of abstract categories greatly differed. Participants were first given the time to explore the exemplars and were let free to manipulate them. Then, they had to sort them in different groups. As predicted, their sorting criteria corresponded more to the experimenters' criteria for concrete than for abstract categories. The sorting criteria used for abstract categories allowed us to divide participants in two further groups: Some of them used a perceptual strategy, thus their sortings differed greatly from the categories defined by the experimenters, while participants of a second group used spatial criteria more similar to the ones that had been defined. Then, half of the participants were taught new labels to design the exemplars and were provided with explanations of the category meaning. Differently from the study by Borghi et al. (2011), in order to enhance the role played by the social input, participants did not read the written category labels and explanations of the category content; rather, labels and explanations were given directly by the experimenter. Because labels and explanations were given in different moments, participants could be divided into early and late language learners. In a further test, they were submitted to a categorical recognition task, i.e., they were required to decide whether two objects belonged to the same category, responding "yes" either with the keyboard or with the microphone (see Fig. 4.5).

The performance with concrete categories was better than that with abstract categories. As predicted, the performance of participants who had received linguistic training was better than the performance of participants who had not.

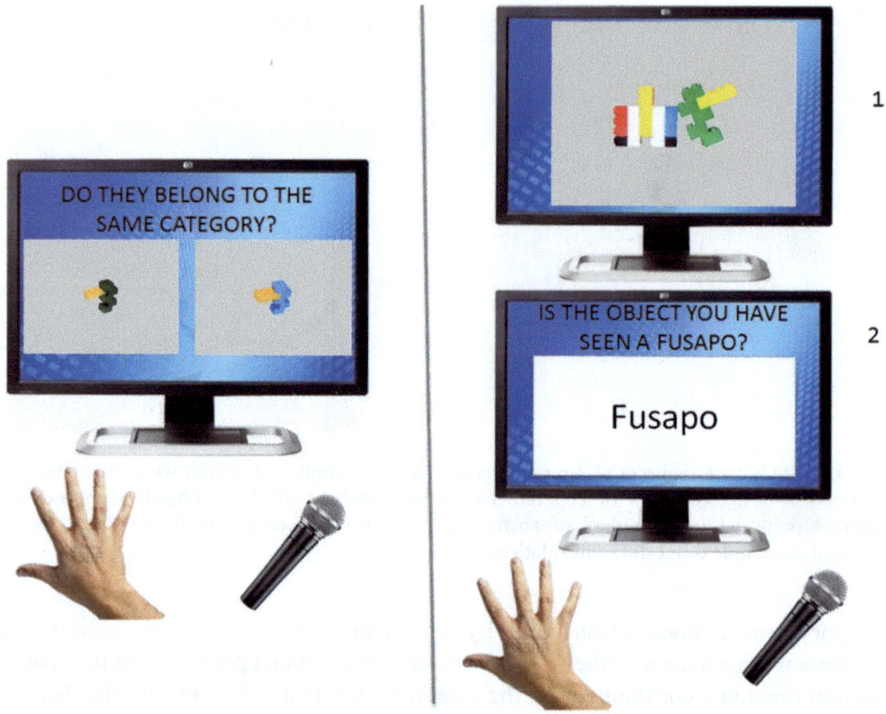

Fig. 4.5 Study by Granito et al. (in preparation). Two of the tasks we used: On the *left* is represented the categorical recognition task, in which participants had to decide whether two objects belonged to the same category, either pressing a "yes" button on keyboard or pronouncing "yes" with the microphone. On the *right* is represented the word-to-picture task: participants saw the image of an object/relation followed by a label and had to press a key on the keyboard or to say "yes" with the microphone if the label designed the relation (abstract) or the object (concrete)

However, this was true for relations, not for objects. This reveals that the acquisition of abstract concepts benefits more than that of concrete categories of the linguistic input. Using language had an effect on body: Participants who did not undergo linguistic training responded faster with the hand than with the mouth, while hand and mouth responses did not differ for participants who were linguistically trained. In addition, linguistically trained participants were faster than non-linguistically trained participants with mouth responses. When all participants were taught labels and explanations, they were submitted to a word-to-picture task: They were presented with the image of a relation followed by a label and had to press a key on the keyboard or to say "yes" with the microphone if the label designed the relation or the object. Among early language learners, participants who had initially employed a perceptual rather than a spatial strategy and responded with the mouth scored better with abstract than with concrete categories, while no difference was present for participants who had used a spatial strategy from the start. This indicates that participants who benefit more from the linguistic help are those whose initial categories are quite distant from those defined by the experimenters and suggests that the role of linguistic input can be modulated not only by the kind of category/word to acquire, but can have a different impact also depending on the strategy subjects use. This is confirmed by the analyses on participants adopting a perceptual strategy: with concrete categories they performed similarly across all conditions, while with abstract categories early language learners scored better with mouth than with hand responses; the opposite was true for late language learners. Finally, late language learners had a worse performance with hand than with mouth responses, while no difference between mouth and hand responses was present for early language learners.

Overall, the two studies provide support to the WAT, in various ways. The first study demonstrates that the different acquisition modality (manipulation vs. observation) has an impact on concrete and abstract categories representation. This impact has a bodily counterpart, as responses with the mouth are faster with abstract than with concrete categories. This effect is particularly marked when not only labels, but explanations of the category meaning are provided as well. This study demonstrates that the linguistic input has a more crucial role for abstract than for concrete categories, and it shows that not only labels, but explanations of the category meaning play a major role. At the same time, our results diverge from the results predicted by theories according to which abstract categories are defined only by linguistic information (e.g., Paivio 1986, 2013). For abstract categories, linguistic information is crucial, but embodied sensorimotor information is crucial as well. Indeed, when explanations are dissociated from perceptual and motor characteristics, the advantage of the mouth over the hand with abstract categories is not present.

The second study complements the first as it provides not only a linguistic input but a social input to word learning as well—labels and explanations are orally given by the experimenter, not by the computer. In addition, to train participants, we used real objects instead of images presented on the computer screen. In this study, we did not manipulate the acquisition modality, but we intended to explore how early or late learning of labels and explanations contribute to the representation of the word meaning, and whether this has an impact on responses performed with different body parts. Overall, results revealed that abstract categories benefited more than concrete ones by early language learning; accordingly, mouth responses were facilitated. In addition, the results of this study suggest that participants might use different categorization strategies. The advantage of linguistic information is particularly marked for those who initially tend to be more perceptually bounded and less sensitive to the relations between elements of a category. Crucially, then, even if the acquisition modality was not manipulated by us, different acquisition modalities emerged: With abstract categories, participants relied more on linguistic input because they needed it; this was particularly true for participants who adopted a perceptual rather than a spatial strategy.

Furthermore, notice that the two studies are complementary also because the way in which concrete and abstract categories are operationalized differs. In the first, concrete categories are defined as categories endowed with a single concrete, manipulable, and perceptually rich referent, while abstract categories are defined as not manipulable, given by more than one referent having complex mutual interactions. In the second, both concrete and abstract categories had manipulable referents or parts, but concrete categories have a single referent composed by many parts, the Lego bricks (e.g., a cup is composed by the container, the handle, etc.), while abstract categories are composed by many objects having different relations (e.g., injustice can be spatially conceptualized as given by one larger element above a smaller one).

4.7 Conclusion: A Possible Acquisition Trajectory

In the developmental literature, an empiricist account as that promoted by Linda Smith and collaborators (Smith 1999, 2000) has typically been contrasted with the socio-pragmatic account. As briefly illustrated, the socio-pragmatic view underlines the importance for word learning of the comprehension of others' intentionality and of sharing perspectives with the others. As we have seen, hybrid approaches propose that the perceptual associative and the social aspects might have a different weight at different ages.

We are not developmental psychologists, thus we do not aim to enter the debate, also because the main points of the debate are outside the aims of the present book. Since abstract words are acquired rather late, the issue of which mechanisms drive early word learning is out of the focus of the WAT view. While the discussion of constraints is of marginal interest for us, for other aspects, we believe that the empiricist, the socio-pragmatic, and the hybrid approaches provide insightful hints that can help provide a basis for the WAT proposal.

In fact, we argue that a similar associative mechanism might work for acquisition of both concrete and abstract words. Perceptive salience, embodied attention and bodily actions would contribute to the success of learning concrete words through associations, eventually aided by parents (Yu and Smith 2012): Children move in their environment, and through selective attention, they get closer and focus on interesting objects, encoding also the similarities and the relationship between them (Wojcik and Saffran 2013). However, for acquiring abstract word, an associative mechanism based on words to referents mapping might be more time consuming and difficult to apply: given the sparse variety of referents abstract words have, children might need a lot of evidence to form a category as, for example, "freedom". This does not mean that an embodied mechanism of referent searching and of selective attention is not present. However, due to the higher difficulty in selecting the perceptual referent, both the social (Tomasello and Akhtar 2000) and the linguistic inputs might be particularly relevant for abstract word learning (Gleitman et al. 2005; Gentner 2006; Wauters et al. 2003). As shown in the acquisition studies by Borghi et al. (2011) and Granito et al. (in preparation), the linguistic input becomes particularly precious since the referents of abstract words are more sparse than those of concrete ones. In addition, words might be associated not only to perceptually salient referents but also to other words, to facilitate learning. This is possible also because, as shown by literature on age of acquisition (Barca et al. 2002), abstract words are acquired rather late compared to concrete ones, when the vocabulary burst has already occurred (Gleitman et al. 2005). Thus, an associative learning mechanism is present both in associating words and referents and words to other words. But, this is not the whole story: in keeping with an embodied perspective, learning of these associations has an impact not only on representation but on the body as well, since different effectors, the mouth and the hand, are activated (Borghi et al. 2011; Granito et al. in preparation).

References

Baldwin, D. (1993). Infants' ability to consult the speaker for clues to word reference. *Journal of Child Language, 2*, 395.

Barca, L., Burani, C., & Arduino, L. S. (2002). Word naming times and psycholinguistic norms for Italian nouns. *Behavior Research Methods Instruments & Computers, 34*(3), 424–434.

Bergen, B. (2012). *Louder than words: The new science of how the mind makes meaning*. New York: Basic Books.

Bergen, B., Narayan, S., & Feldman, J. (2003). Embodied verbal semantics: evidence from an image-verb matching task. *Proceedings of the Twenty-Fifth Annual Conference of the Cognitive Science Society.*

Birch, S., Vauthier, S., & Bloom, P. (2008). Three- and four-year-olds spontaneously use others' past performance to guide their learning. *Cognition, 107*, 1018–1034.

Borghi, A. M., Flumini, A., Cimatti, F., Marocco, D., & Scorolli, C. (2011). Manipulating objects and telling words: A study on concrete and abstract words acquisition. *Frontiers in Psychology, 2*, 15. doi:10.3389/fpsyg.2011.00015

Bruner, J. S. (1990). *Acts of meaning*. Harvard: Harvard University Press.

Bruner, J. S. (1983). *Child's talk: Learning to use language*. New York: Norton.

Corriveau, K., & Harris, P. L. (2009). Choosing your informant: Weighing familiarity and recent accuracy. *Developmental Science, 12*(3), 426–437.

Gelman, S. A. (2009). Learning from others: Children's construction of concepts. *Annual Review of Psychology, 60*, 115–140.

Gentner, D. (2006). Why verbs are hard to learn. In K. Hirsch-Pasek & R. Golinkoff (Eds.), *Action meets words: How children learn verbs* (pp. 544–564). New York: Oxford University Press.

Gergely, G., Nádasdy, Z., Csibra, G., & Bíró, S. (1995). Taking the intentional stance at 12 months of age. *Cognition, 56*(2), 165–193.

Gillette, J., Gleitman, H., Gleitman, L. R., & Lederer, A. (1999). Human simulations of vocabulary learning. *Cognition, 73*, 135–176.

Gleitman, L. R., Cassidy, K., Papafragou, A., Nappa, R., & Trueswell, J. T. (2005). Hard words. *Journal of Language Learning and Development, 1*(1), 23–64.

Golinkoff, R. M., & Hirsh-Pasek, K. (2006). Baby Wordsmith: From associationist to social sophisticate. *Current Directions in Psychological Science, 15*, 30–34.

Gomez, R. L., & Gerken, L. (1999). Artificial grammar learning by 1-year-olds leads to specific and abstract knowledge. *Cognition, 70*, 109–135.

Gómez, R. L., & Gerken, L. A. (2000). Infant artificial language learning and language acquisition. *Trends in Cognitive Science, 4*(5), 178–186.

Granito, C., Scorolli, C., & Borghi, A.M. (in preparation). Alice in Legoland: A study on abstract words acquisition.

Harris, P. L., & Koenig, M. A. (2006). Trust in testimony: How children learn about science and religion. *Child Development, 77*, 505–524.

Henrich, J., Heine, S. J., & Norenzayan, A. (2010). The weirdest people in the world? *Behavioral and Brain Sciences, 33*, 61–83. doi:10.1017/S0140525X0999152X

Hirsh-Pasek, K., Golinkoff, R. M., Hennon, E. A., & Maguire, M. J. (2004). Hybrid theories at the frontier of developmental psychology: The emergentist coalition model of word learning as a case in point. In D. Geoffrey Hall & S. R. Waxman (Eds.), *Weaving a lexicon* (pp. 173–204). Cambridge, MA: MIT Press.

Hirsh-Pasek, K., Golinkoff, R. M., & Hollich, G. (2000). An emergentist coalition model for word learning: Mapping words to objects is a product of the interaction of multiple cues. In R. M. Golinkoff, K. Hirsh-Pasek, L. Bloom, L. B. Smith, A. L. Woodard, N. Akhtar, M. Tomasello, & G. Hollich (Eds.), *Becoming a word learner: A debate on lexical acquisition* (pp. 179–186). New York: Oxford University Press.

Hollich, G., Hirsh-Pasek, K., & Golinkoff, R.M. (2000). *Breaking the language barrier: An emergentist coalition model for the origins of word learning*. Society for Research in Child Development Monograph Series. Chicago: University of Chicago Press.

Jaakkola, R. O., & Slaughter, V. (2002). Children's body knowledge: Understanding 'life' as a biological goal. *British Journal of Developmental Psychology, 20*, 325–342.

Karpov, Y. V., & Bransford, J. D. (1995). LS Vygotsky and the doctrine of empirical and theoretical learning. *Educational Psychologist, 30*(2), 61–66.

Landau, B., Smith, L. B., & Jones, S. S. (1988). The importance of shape in early lexical learning. *Cognitive Development, 3*, 299–321.

Lany, J., & Saffran, J. R. (2010). From statistics to meaning: Infants, acquisition of lexical categories. *Psychological Science, 21*(2), 284–291. doi:10.1177/0956797609358570

Markman, E. (1989). *Categorization and naming in young children*. Cambridge, MA: MIT Press.

Medin, D. L., & Atran, S. (2004). The native mind: Biological categorization and reasoning in development and across cultures. *Psychological Review, 111*, 960–983.

Medina, T. N., Snedeker, J., Trueswell, J. C., & Gleitman, L. R. (2011). How words can and cannot be learned by observation. *Proceedings of the National Academy of Sciences, 108*, 9014–9019.

Nelson, K. (1988). Constraints on word learning? *Cognitive Development, 3*, 221–236.

Nisbett, R. E. (2003). *The geography of thought*. New York: Free Press.

Nisbett, R. E., Peng, K., Choi, I., & Norenzayan, A. (2001). Culture and systems of thought: Holistic versus analytic cognition. *Psychological Review, 108*(2), 291–310. doi:10.1037/0033-295X.108.2.291. PMID 11381831.

Paivio, A. (1986). Mental representations: A dual coding approach. New York: Oxford University.

Paivio, A. (2013). Dual coding theory, word abstractness, and emotion: A critical review of Kousta et al. (2011). *Journal of Experimental Psychology,* General, *142*(1), 282–7. doi: 10.1037/a0027004.

Prinz, J. (2012). *Beyond human nature: How culture and experience shape our lives*. London, Penguin, New York: Norton.

Pruden, S. M., Hirsh-Pasek, K., Golinkoff, R. M., & Hennon, E. A. (2006). The birth of words: Ten-month-olds learn words through perceptual salience. *Child Development, 77*(2), 266–280.

Romberg, A. R., & Saffran, J. R. (2010). Statistical learning and language acquisition. *Wiley Interdisciplinary Review: Cognitive Science, 1*(6), 906–914.

Sabbagh, M. A., & Baldwin, D. A. (2001). Learning words from knowledgeable versus ignorant speakers: Links between preschoolers' theory of mind and semantic development. *Child Development, 72*, 1054–1070.

Saffran, J. R., Aslin, R. N., & Newport, E. L. (1996). Statistical learning by 8-month-old infants. *Science, 274*, 1926–1928.

Shweder, R. (1991). *Thinking through cultures*. Harvard University Press.

Smith, L. B. (1999). Children's noun learning: How general learning processes make specialized learning mechanisms. In B. MacWhinney (Ed.), *The emergence of language* (pp. 227–305). Mahwah, New Jersey: Erlbaum.

Smith, L. B. (2000). Learning how to learn words: An associative crane. In R. M. Golinkoff, K. Hirsh-Pasek, L. Bloom, L. Smith, A. Woodward, N. Akhtar, M. Tomasello, & G. Hollich (Eds.), *Becoming a word learner: A debate on lexical acquisition*. New York, NY: Oxford University Press.

Smith, L. B. (2005). Action alters shape categories. *Cognitive Science, 29*, 665–679.

Smith, L. B., & Yu, C. (2008). Infants rapidly learn word-referent mappings via cross-situational statistics. *Cognition, 106*(3), 1558–1568.

Snedeker, J., & Gleitman, L. (2004). Why it is hard to label our concepts? In D. G. Hall & S. R. Waxman (Eds.), *Weaving a Lexicon* (pp. 603–636). Cambridge, MA: MIT Press.

Tizard, B., & Hughes, M. (1984). *Young children learning*. London: Fontana.

Tomasello, M. (1992). The social basis of language acquisition. *Social Development, 1*(1), 67–87.

Tomasello, M. (2000). First steps toward a usage-based theory of language acquisition. *Cognitive Linguistics, 11*(1–2), 61–82.

Tomasello, M., & Akhtar, N. (1995). Two-year-olds use pragmatic cues to differentiate reference to objects and actions. *Cognitive Development, 10*, 201–224.

Tomasello, M., & Akhtar, N. (2000). Five questions for any theory of word learning. In R. M. Golinkoff, K. Hirsh-Pasek, L. Bloom, L. B. Smith, A. L. Woodward, N. Akhtar, M. Tomasello, & G. Hollich (Eds.), *Becoming a word learner: A debate on lexical acquisition* (pp. 179–186). New York: Oxford University Press.

Tomasello, M., Carpenter, M., Call, J., Behne, T., & Moll, H. (2005). Understanding and sharing intentions: The origins of cultural cognition. *Behavioral and Brain Sciences, 28*, 675–691.

Vosniadou, S. (1994). Universal and culture-specific properties of children's mental models of the earth. In L. A. Hirschfeld & S. A. Gelman (Eds.), *Mapping the mind: Domain specificity in cognition and culture* (pp. 412–430). New York: Cambridge University Press.

Vygotsky, L. S. (1978). *Mind in society*. Cambridge, MA: Harvard University Press.

Vygotsky, L.S. (1981) The genesis of higher mental functions. In J. V. Wertsch (Ed.), *The concept of activity in Soviet psychology*. Armonk, NY: Sharpe.

Vygotsky, L. S. (1986). *Thought and language*. Cambridge, MA: MIT Press.

Vygotsky, L. S. (1987). Thinking and speech. In R. W. Rieber & A. S. Carton (Eds.), *The collected works of L. S. Vygotsky, Volume 1: Problems of general psychology,* (Trans. N. Minick). New York: Plenum.

Wauters, L. N., Tellings, A. E. J. M., van Bon, W. H. J., & Mak, W. M. (2008). Mode of acquisition as a factor in deaf children's reading comprehension. *Journal of Deaf Studies and Deaf Education, 13*(2), 175–192.

Wauters, L. N., Tellings, A. E. J. M., van Bon, W. H. J., & van Haaften, A. W. (2003). Mode of acquisition of word meanings: The viability of a theoretical construct. *Applied Psycholinguistics, 24*, 385–406.

Weizman, Z. O., & Snow, C. E. (2001). Lexical output as related to children's vocabulary acquisition: Effects of sophisticated exposure and support for meaning. *Developmental Psychology, 37*(2), 265–279. doi:10.1037/0012-1649.37.2.265

Wojcik, E. H., & Saffran, J. R. (2013). The ontogeny of lexical networks: Toddlers encode the relationships among referents when learning novel words? *Psychological Science, 24*(10), 1898–1905.

Woodward, A. L., Markman, E., & Fitzsimmons, C. M. (1994). Rapid word learning in 13- and 18-month-olds. *Developmental Psychology, 30*, 553–556.

Yu, C., & Smith, L. B. (2007). Rapid word learning under uncertainty via cross-situational statistics. *Psychological Science, 18*(5), 414–420.

Yu, C., & Smith, L. B. (2012). Embodied attention and word learning by toddlers. *Cognition, 125*, 244–262.

Chapter 5
What Can Neuroscience Tell Us About Abstract Concepts

> *To be an abstract painter does not mean to abstract from naturally occurring opportunities for comparison, but, quite apart from such opportunities, to distil pure pictorial relations: light to dark, colour to light and dark, colour to colour, long to short, broad to narrow, sharp to dull, left–right, above–below, behind–in front, circle to square to triangle.*
>
> Paul Klee

5.1 Concreteness Effect

Concreteness is a critical organizing factor in semantic memory, and recognition of the discrepancy between abstract and concrete concepts has a long history in psychology and philosophy (Locke 1685). Behavioral differences in processing between abstract and concrete concepts have been well documented and referred to as the concreteness effect: Concrete words are acquired earlier and are remembered and recognized more rapidly than abstract words (Kroll and Merves 1986; Schwanenflugel 1991). There are quite numerous studies addressing the issue of processing of abstract and concrete concepts in normal subjects and patients. There is a broad evidence that concrete words are more quickly recognized (Strain et al. 1995; Kroll and Merves 1986; James 1975), better remembered (Paivio 1971), and more resilient to brain damage (Katz and Goodglass 1990; Roeltgen et al. 1983; Coltheart et al. 1987; Goodglass et al. 1969) than abstract words. It is a common clinical knowledge that patients with specific cortical lesions who have acquired language deficits most commonly experience greater impairments with abstract words than concrete words, but the lesions associated with this deficit do not have a consistent localization (Coltheart 1980; Katz and Goodglass 1990; Martin and Saffran 1992; Goodglass et al. 1969; Saffran and Martin 1990). The concreteness effect is increased in patients with aphasia caused by left-hemispheric damage (Goodglass et al. 1969) and dyslexia (Shallice and Warrington 1975). On average, patients recovering from aphasia regain much faster the access to concrete words and sentences, whereas the understanding of more abstract and more complex words and sentences is much longer impaired and requires a much more intensive therapy. We observed quite recently the concreteness effects in the domain of writing in a patient with chronic non-fluent aphasia. This patient had a good to moderate recovery of her language communication skills and could re-learn writing with her non-paretic left hand. She had no

A. M. Borghi and F. Binkofski, *Words as Social Tools: An Embodied View on Abstract Concepts*, SpringerBriefs in Cognition,
DOI: 10.1007/978-1-4614-9539-0_5, © The Author(s) 2014

problems with writing of words like "ball" or "car." When asked to write the word "freedom," she repeated the word verbally and said that it should be very easy to write it down. But, instead she drew only a line, which could have been the beginning of the first letter and then stopped. The same happened any time the patients attempted to write words with abstract content and with low imageability. Such condition was described already by Bub and Kertesz (1982) and named deep agraphia. In the domain of reading, a deficit in reading aloud abstract words is the prototypic characteristic of deep dyslexic patients. Patients with deep dyslexia are much more able to read aloud words with a concrete or better an imageable, meaning than those with an abstract meaning (Shallice and Warrington 1975; Coltheart et al. 1987). It is much easier to read "thing" than to read "thought". There is a general agreement that the phonological route or routes for reading are inoperative in patients with deep dyslexia. Shallice and Cooper (2013) propose that it would seem straightforward to produce an explanation for the inability to read abstract words in deep dyslexia patients which is based on the assumption that there are different systems for holding the semantic representations of abstract and imageable/concrete words. According to the authors, if one assumes that there is an at least partial separability between the semantic systems holding representations of imageable and abstract words, then it is simple to assume that in this functional syndrome, the latter subsystem is no longer directly accessible from a visual word-form system, while the former subsystem is.

5.2 Reversed Concreteness Effect in Patients with Deep Dyslexia and Herpes Encephalitis

A reverse concreteness effect (Warrington 1975), showing a more severe impairment in the understanding of concrete rather than abstract concepts, has been found in patients with semantic dementia (Breedin et al. 1994; Reilly et al. 2006). The patient described by Breedin had a progressive semantic loss due to atrophic changes in his temporal lobes, particularly on the left. His semantic impairment predominantly involved object terms, with relative sparing of abstract nouns and most aspects of verb meaning. The patient showed an advantage for abstract words on a wide range of tasks (e.g., producing definitions, synonymy judgments). These findings challenged accounts that attributed the concreteness effect to a quantitative superiority at the level of the underlying conceptual representations. Apparently, there were qualitative differences between abstract and concrete concepts. The authors proposed that concrete concepts depended more on perceptual attributes that were disproportionately impaired in their patient. They further proposed that perceptual components of semantic representations are associated with structures in the inferior temporal lobe(s) (Breedin et al. 1994). This reversed concreteness effect can be observed in only a small number of patients. Recently, Bonner et al. (2009) reviewed the reports in which a reversal of the concreteness effect—a specific deficit for concrete words leaving abstract words intact—have been described (reviewed by Bonner et al. 2009). Bonner and colleagues (2009) identified 11 patients with semantic dementia who exhibited the reversal of the concreteness effect, specifically with visual-based stimuli, and located their peak neurological degeneration to a portion of the ventral surface of the anterior temporal lobes. This region is commonly affected in semantic dementia; however, the reversal of the concreteness effect is quite rare in these patients (Hoffman and Lambon Ralph 2011).

This double dissociation between the concreteness effect (for example, in deep dyslexia) and the reversed concreteness effect in semantic dementia suggests a difference in neural representation of abstract and concrete concepts. One possible explanation of the concreteness effect is the difference in imageability between abstract and concrete concepts. Concrete concepts have higher imageability than abstract concepts: For example, "hammer" is more easily visualized than "freedom." The engagement of mental imagery in semantic concept processing has been argued to contribute to the difference in abstract and concrete concepts representation (Marschark et al. 1987; Paivio 1991). Mental imagery is similar to a perceptual experience, but happens without the presence of external stimuli (Jeannerod 2001).

The issue of imageability of abstract and concrete concepts has been addressed recently in more depth (see Chap. 1). Imageability is typically defined as the ease to which a word can evoke a visual image, while concreteness typically refers to whether the concept itself is situated in time and space (see for example, Paivio 1967). These variables are conceptually related and tightly correlated with each other (e.g., imageability can account for 72 % of the variability in concreteness, see Kousta et al. 2011), but nevertheless distinct. Kousta et al. 2011 demonstrated that when imageability is controlled between abstract and concrete words, the concreteness effect disappears and in fact, abstract words are processed more quickly than concrete words. But, despite the recent findings, the data on the concreteness effect and the reversed concreteness effect obtained in patients indicate unequivocally at least partial parallel processing of abstract and concrete concepts. The question arises whether neuroimaging data can help to get a clearer picture.

5.3 Neuroimaging of Abstract and Concrete Concepts and Mental Imagery

In order to understand language function in both healthy and clinical populations, several brain imaging studies addressed the issue of representation of abstract and concrete concepts in the brain. The most basic question toward neuroimaging in the current context is whether abstract and concrete concepts are represented in the same brain areas, or whether they have separate representations. Or maybe they share some representations and have some specific representations beyond that. Data on patients, as described above, suggest that at least the last option should be valid. As mentioned before, one possible explanation of the concreteness effect is the difference in imageability between abstract and concrete concepts (see Chap. 1 for further discussion on this). In general, concrete concepts have higher imageability than abstract concepts: For example, "hammer" is more easily visualized than "freedom". Representation of abstract and concrete concepts is supported by mental imagery, which is involved in semantic concept processing (Marschark et al. 1987; Paivio 1991). It has been proposed that mental imagery is based on perceptual and motor simulations and is similar to a perceptual experience (Jeannerod 2001). Accordingly, mental imagery activates modality-specific sensory or sensorimotor systems (Binkofski et al. 2000; Borst and Kosslyn 2008; Farah 1995; Jeannerod and Decety 1995), which indicates that imagery and perception or action share common neural mechanisms (Jeannerod 1995). Perceptual symbol systems theory postulates that all concepts are grounded in action, perceptual, and emotional experience; language comprehension could also be interpreted as the construction of perceptual and motor simulation (Barsalou 1999, 2003; Barsalou et al. 2003). Another suggestion is that mental imagery may rely on the mechanism of reenactment (Halpern and Zatorre 1999; Jeannerod and Decety 1995; Gallese 2003), which is viewed as underlying conceptualization and comprehension (Barsalou 1999).

As discussed in Chap. 3, a central question in the debate of whether processing mechanisms of abstract and concrete concepts differ is whether concepts are represented by words or by non-language factors, such as perceptual and motor experiences. The classical dual-coding hypothesis suggests a common verbal representation for both concrete and abstract concepts and an additional mental imagery process for concrete concepts (Paivio 1991). From a neural perspective, dual-coding theory predicts that representation of concrete concepts is based more on neural substrates of the imagery processing system compared with abstract concepts. On the other hand, the concreteness effect can also be interpreted without incorporating mental imagery. The context availability theory argues that representational information and connections to semantic knowledge lead to richer context, resulting in more efficient processing of concrete concepts in comparison with abstract concepts (Schwanenflugel et al. 1988).

In the context of the theoretical considerations, it is worthwhile to have a closer look at the results of neuroimaging studies on abstract and concrete concepts. To date, results of these studies have been inconsistent. Some studies have found greater activations for concrete compared to abstract concepts only (Mestres-Missè et al. 2008; Wise et al. 2000). Specifically, imagery-based and perceptual regions were reported to be activated for concrete more than abstract contrast in several studies (Binder et al. 2005; Fiebach and Friederici 2004; Grossman et al. 2002). Mental imagery generation activated either predominantly right hemisphere (Paivio 1991) or left hemisphere (D'Esposito et al. 1997), or bilateral areas (Binder et al. 2005). Some earlier studies only identified areas with greater activation for abstract compared to concrete concepts (Friederici et al. 2000; Grossman et al.

2002; Jesssen et al. 2000; Kiehl et al. 1999; Noppeney and Price 2004; Perani et al. 1999; Pexman et al. 2007; Rüschemeyer et al. 2007). There were, however, also some more recent studies that found activations of brain areas dedicated either to processing of concrete or abstract language (Binder et al. 2005; Fiebach and Friederici 2004; Fliessbach et al. 2006; Harris et al. 2006; Sabsevitz et al. 2005; Tettamanti et al. 2008; Wallentin et al. 2005; Whatmough et al. 2004; Sakreida et al. 2013).

For example, in the study of Binder et al. (2005), concrete and abstract words, and relative to non-words, both activated a left-lateralized network of multimodal association areas previously linked with verbal semantic processing. Areas in the left lateral temporal lobe were equally activated by both word types, whereas bilateral regions including the angular gyrus and the dorsal prefrontal cortex were more strongly engaged by concrete words. Relative to concrete words, abstract words activated left inferior frontal regions previously linked with phonological and verbal working memory processes. The authors propose that there are overlapping but partly distinct neural systems for processing concrete and abstract concepts. Binder et al. (2005) also suggested that the stronger left inferior frontal gyrus activation reflects the additional semantic processing for abstract words compared to concrete words during a lexical decision task, as abstract words are held in working memory in phonological form to a greater degree than concrete words.

Similar results with respect to abstract concepts were found by Desai et al. (2010) in an magnetic resonance imaging (fMRI) study, in which the participants listened to sentences describing hand/arm action events, visual events, or abstract behaviors. In comparison with visual and abstract sentences, areas associated with planning and control of hand movements, motion perception, and vision were activated when understanding sentences describing actions. Sensorimotor areas were activated to a greater extent also for sentences with actions that relied mostly on hands, as opposed to arms. Visual sentences activated a small area in the secondary visual cortex, whereas abstract sentences activated superior temporal and inferior frontal regions. The results support the view that abstract concepts are processed in the semantic system, whereas linguistic understanding of actions partly involves imagery or simulation of actions and relies on some of the same neural substrate used for planning, performing, and perceiving actions.

On the search for the semantic system in the human brain, Binder et al. (2009) performed a metaanalysis of a large number of imaging studies using the method of activation likelihood estimate (ALE). The resulting activations formed a distinct, left-lateralized network which comprised 7 regions: posterior inferior parietal lobe, middle temporal gyrus, fusiform and parahippocampal gyri, dorsomedial prefrontal cortex, inferior frontal gyrus, ventromedial prefrontal cortex, and posterior cingulate gyrus. According to Binder, the cortical regions involved in semantic processing can be grouped into three broad categories: posterior multimodal and heteromodal association cortex, heteromodal prefrontal cortex, and medial limbic regions. In the context of our book, the most interesting subcontrast involved the distinction between perceptually encoded knowledge (i.e., knowledge of concrete objects derived from sensorimotor experience) and verbally encoded knowledge (i.e., knowledge acquired through language) (Paivio 1986). Whereas the overlap for the ''perceptual'' foci occurred in the angular gyrus bilaterally, left mid-fusiform gyrus, left DMPFC, and left posterior cingulate, significant overlap for the ''verbal'' foci occurred in the left IFG (mainly pars orbitalis) and left anterior superior temporal sulcus (STS). These results confirmed the involvement of these areas in the processing of abstract concepts.

Similar results for processing of abstract concepts were reported by another large metaanalysis performed by Wang et al. (2010), where abstract concepts elicited greater activity in the inferior frontal gyrus and middle temporal gyrus compared to concrete concepts, while concrete concepts elicit greater activity in the posterior cingulate, precuneus, fusiform gyrus, and parahippocampal gyrus compared to abstract concepts. These results provide one more hint toward greater engagement of the verbal system for processing of abstract concepts and greater engagement of the perceptual system for processing of concrete concepts.

The left inferior frontal gyrus has also been implicated in phonological processing during working memory tasks (Fiebach and Friederici 2004). Lesions to the left IFG produce deficits in phonological and syntactic processes (Bookheimer 2002; Caramazza et al. 1981). Sabsevitz et al. (2005) proposed that activation in the more posterior parts of the frontal lobe by abstract concepts may represent phonological working memory processing, while the more anterior regions of the inferior frontal gyrus may play a role in the putative verbal semantic system. These inferences suggest that neural representational differences between abstract and concrete concepts might also be ascribed to phonological processing differences caused by different levels of semantic processing difficulties. Left middle temporal gyrus has been shown to play a role in several aspects of language processing, including processing of abstract concepts (Pexman et al. 2007). Noppeney and Price (2004) attributed the difference in left middle temporal gyrus activation between abstract and concrete concepts to distinct retrieval mechanisms or strategies, rather than different neural representations or processing demands.

Wiemer-Hastings et al. (2001) (see also Barsalou 2003) proposed that there is a kind of continuous transition between concrete and abstract concepts. Concrete concepts have some abstract features and vice versa (see also Chap. 1). We tested this notions in an fMRI study in which we asked participants to read simple sentences, which combined each concrete noun with an adequate concrete verb and an adequate abstract verb, as well as an adequate abstract noun with either kind of verbs previously used (see also a behavioral and a TMS studies by Scorolli et al. 2011, 2012, in which the same stimuli and paradigm were used). Thus, our experimental design included a continuum from pure concreteness to mere abstractness (e.g., to grasp/to describe—a flower/a concept) (Sakreida et al. 2013) (see Fig. 5.1).

As expected, comprehension of both concrete and abstract language content activated the core areas of the sensorimotor neural network, namely the left lateral (precentral gyrus) and medial (supplementary motor area) premotor cortex. While the purely concrete multiword expressions elicited activations within the left

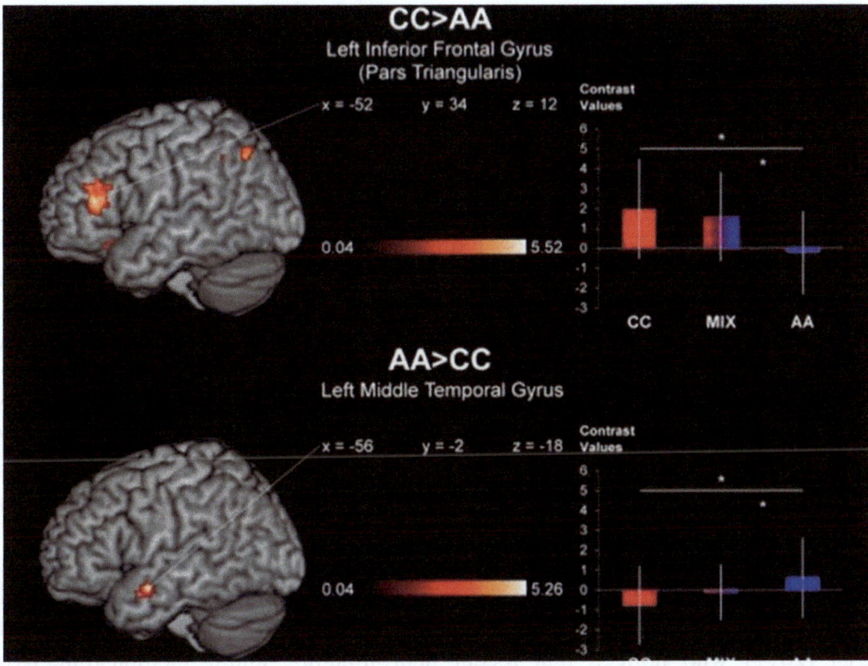

Fig. 5.1 Study by Sakreida et al. (2013), results from fMRI. Demonstrated are differences between brain activations during processing of concrete noun–verb combinations (*top panel*) compared to abstract noun–verb combinations (*bottom panel*) and extracted contrast values for the pure abstract, the summarized mixed conditions and the pure abstract conditions. Notice the highest level of activation in the *left* posterior inferior frontal gyrus and inferior parietal cortex for the most concrete sentences and in the *left middle* temporal cortex for the most abstract sentences. The mixed (abstract–concrete, concrete–abstract) sentences produce activation levels in between. The results are in favor of a continuum between the representation of concrete and abstract words

inferior frontal gyrus (pars triangularis) and two foci within the left inferior parietal cortex, the purely abstract multiword expressions were represented in the anterior part of left middle temporal gyrus that is part of the language processing system. Conform with our hypothesis, the strengths of activation varied with the grade of concreteness/abstractness. At the site of the strongest activation related to concrete stimuli, there was a weaker activation by combined abstract/concrete contrasts and correspondingly there was also some weaker activation by mixed contrasts at the site of strongest abstract activation (Sakreida et al. 2013).

The idea of a continuum between concrete and abstract representation of language was also followed by Weiss and Mueller (2013). In their investigation of long-range EEG coherence, they found that processing of concrete and abstract sentences relies both on common and different neuronal networks. Concrete language was consistently associated with a higher coherence, proposing the involvement of more neuronal resources for mental sensorimotor simulation processes. The authors also concluded that concrete and abstract languages are processed along an analog continuum and are not strictly separated with respect to their amount and quality of mental simulations. This study further supports the view proposed by embodied and grounded theories that sensorimotor systems are modulated by not only the comprehension of concrete but also partly of abstract language (e.g., Glenberg et al. 2008; Scorolli et al. 2011).

Taken together, the consistent activation across studies resulting from processing of abstract compared to concrete concepts in left-hemispheric areas, especially the inferior frontal gyurs, is linked to activation elicited by a language-based or verbal system. Representation of abstract concepts may be held in working memory to a greater degree and require more efforts of semantic retrieval. This is in line with the hypothesis formulated by WAT according to which abstract concepts activate more the linguistic networks. However, this is not the end of the story, since WAT predicts that both concrete and abstract words activate the sensorimotor network and the distributed network associated with their meaning/content. This is supported by a recent study, which showed that brain regions underlying mentalizing and social cognition (e.g., medial prefrontal cortex, STS) were activated during the processing of the abstract concept "to convince," whereas brain regions underlying numerical cognition (e.g., bilateral intraparietal sulcus) were activated to represent the concept "arithmetic" (Wilson-Mendenhall et al. 2013). This is also in line with the recent conceptual work by Binder and Desai (2011) who noticed that recent neuroimaging studies demonstrate two striking results: the participation of modality-specific sensory, motor and emotion systems in language comprehension, and the existence of large brain regions that participate in comprehension tasks but are not modality-specific. These latter regions, which include the inferior parietal lobe and much of the temporal lobe, lie at convergences of multiple perceptual processing streams. These convergences enable increasingly abstract, supramodal representations of perceptual experience that support a varicty of conceptual functions including object recognition, social cognition, and language (Binder and Desai 2011).

5.4 Neuroimaging of Abstract and Concrete Concepts and Emotional Valence

Despite these results are promising and partially converging, they must be interpreted with caution. It is important to note that there are large inconsistencies between individual studies; thus, it is difficult to identify cortical regions specific to processing abstract conceptual knowledge. One explanation for these disparate findings is that important stimulus dimensions were not controlled in the tested abstract concepts.

An important advancement in studying the representational foundations of abstract concepts is the idea that abstract concepts may be grounded, or embodied, in affective meaning. The affective embodiment account suggests that while concrete words are learned and understood through sensorimotor referents, abstract words are learned and understood through emotional referents and that emotional valence is a key component of abstract conceptualization (Vigliocco et al. 2009). The affective embodiment account reminds that prior research did not control for a key confounding variable: imageability. Most research in this field covaries imageability with concreteness because these two variables are tightly linked, but they have some distinctions. Imageability is typically defined as the ease to which a word can evoke a visual image, while concreteness typically refers to whether the concept itself is situated in time and space (see for example, Paivio, 1967). As described in Chap. 1, these variables are conceptually related and tightly correlated with each other (e.g., imageability can account for 72 % of the variability in concreteness, see Koustaet al. 2011), but nevertheless distinct. And again, Kousta and colleagues demonstrated that when imageability is controlled between abstract and concrete words, the concreteness effect disappears and interestingly, abstract words are processed more quickly than concrete words (Kousta et al. 2011). We also did not find evidence for concreteness effect with sentences: in both Scorolli et al. 2011 (behavioral) and 2012 (TMS) studies, we found that compatible combinations of simple sentences (concrete–concrete; abstract–abstract) were faster than mixed combinations (concrete–abstract; abstract–concrete); thus, no advantage of concrete elements per se was found.

The affective embodiment account suggests that three kinds of information contribute to semantic knowledge: sensorimotor, affective, and linguistic (Vigliocco et al. 2009). What ultimately divides abstract words from concrete words is that abstract words are more dependent on affective and emotional information, and concrete words are more dependent upon sensorimotor information, and both rely on linguistic information to some degree. According to this model, imageability is related, but ultimately independent, and failure to control for imageability in studies of concreteness have led to inconsistent findings. Emotional valence, in this model, works as a function of abstractness and cannot be controlled without losing some essence of abstract meaning. The decision to control for one variable, and not the other, has obvious implications for behavioral research, as demonstrated by the absence and so-called reversal of the concreteness effect found by Kousta and colleagues (2011). In a recent study, subjects were asked to carry out a lexical decision task on abstract and concrete words while undergoing an fMRI scan (Vigliocco et al. 2013). The abstract and concrete words were tightly controlled on an impressive range of lexical and sublexical variables, including imageability. The results of a subtraction analysis indicated that recognition of abstract concepts was associated with activations in one region: the rostral anterior cingulate cortex (rACC). Within the rACC alone, BOLD activity was modulated by hedonic valence. The authors argue that this evinces that abstract concepts are grounded in affective experience while concrete concepts are grounded in sensorimotor experience and that this has a neurological basis.

This very interesting finding was questioned, however, in a very recent study by Skipper and Olson (in press), who argue that in the Vigliocco et al. (2013) study, the abstract words were significantly more valenced than the concrete words.

The authors offer an alternative explanation for this finding, arguing that the rACC was responding to emotional valence rather than abstract concepts per se. As the rostral and ventral aspects of the ACC are part of paralimbic cortex (Bush Luu and Posner 2000) they play a specific role in social and emotional processes, such as monitoring behavioral expectations (Apps Balsters and Ramnani 2012), processing of social emotional tasks (Lane et al. 1998; Castelli et al. 2000, 2002) or of emotional Stroop task (Whalen et al. 1998). In their own imaging study, Skipper and Olson examined whether abstract verbal stimuli activate cortical regions overlapping with those activated by emotional stimuli, while carefully controlling emotional valence across the abstract and concrete stimuli. As in many previous studies (for example Binder et al. 2005; Sakreida et al. 2013), they found overlapping activations for abstract and concrete contrasts. These contrasts overlapped in the left temporal pole, in the left posterior middle temporal gyrus, in the medial orbito-frontal cortex and medial occipital cortex, and in the posterior STS. Areas that responded uniquely to concrete concepts were found in the left inferior surface of the anterior temporal lobe, posterior cingulate cortex, and medial superior frontal cortex. Regions that remained exclusively responsive to abstract concepts were found only in the right STS and right temporal pole. A region of interests analysis revealed that the rACC was responsive to valence, not to abstractness, when concreteness and valence were unconfounded.

The results of the last two contradicting studies are especially interesting. The study by Vigliocco et al. (2013) demonstrates that when the stimuli are balanced for many parameters, especially for imageability, then most brain activations reported in previous studies vanish. The rACC activation reported in this study can indeed be explained by the higher emotional valence of the abstract words. This notion is confirmed by the results of the study by Skipper and Olson, who did not found an rACC activation by abstract stimuli, when they are balanced for emotional valence. But, there is also another interesting conclusion that can be drawn from both studies: they underpin the influence of imageability and maybe emotional valence on the patterns of activations found in many previous studies. As presented in the patients' data and by Kousta et al. (2011), imageability could be responsible for the concreteness effect, which helps many patients with aphasia to understand concrete concepts more easily than abstract ones. On the other hand, emotional valence could be responsible for the reversed concreteness effect in semantic dementia.

5.5 Conclusion: Hints from Neuroscience

The concreteness and the reversed concreteness effect observed in patients with different pathology and with different location of brain lesions indicate a double dissociation of these effects. On the other hand, they demonstrate that concrete and abstract concepts are processed, at least partially, in parallel. One important factor in the concreteness effect is imageability of the perceived concepts, because careful control for imageability can abolish the concreteness effect or even lead to its reversion. The literature on imaging of processing abstract and concrete concepts is inconsistent. But one conclusion from imaging is almost certain: Processing of abstract and concrete concepts share neural representations which contain also sensorimotor areas. The issue of whether specific representations for abstract and concrete concepts exist is far more difficult, since some studies report more activations of left-hemispheric areas and some others report right lateralized activations for abstract concepts. However, there is growing evidence that the semantic system is involved in the processing of abstract words. This is consistent with the WAT approach, according to which abstract concepts activate more the linguistic networks. WAT predicts also that both concrete and abstract words activate the sensorimotor network and the distributed network associated with their meaning/content. The origin of the difference in the reported activations can be the different imageability and emotion valence of the stimuli used. But, on the other hand, imageability and emotional valence of concepts can be the origin of the concreteness and reversed concreteness effect in patients. Further research is needed in order to determine whether, as hypothesized by WAT, the different neural representation of abstract and concrete concepts depend at least in part from their different kind of acquisition modality.

A further intriguing possibility, in line with the idea of a continuum, is that more subtle differences between different subtypes of abstract concepts exist. This would require more fine-grained analyses of the features abstract concepts activate, as well as the exploration of their corresponding different kinds of neural representation and different effects in patients [for some recent studies in this direction, see the study on a patient with global aphasia by Crutch et al. (2013) and the behavioral study by Ghio et al. (2013).

References

Apps, M. A., Balsters, J. H., & Ramnani, N. (2012). The anterior cingulate cortex: Monitoring the outcomes of others ' decisions. *Social Neuroscience, 7*(4), 424–435.

Barsalou, L. W. (1999). Perceptual symbol systems. *Behavioral and Brain Sciences, 22*, 577–660.

Barsalou, L. W. (2003). Abstraction in perceptual symbol systems. *Philosophical Transactions of the Royal Society of London. Series B: Biological Sciences, 358*, 1177–1187.

Barsalou, L. W., Simmons, W. K., Barbey, A. K., & Wilson, C. D. (2003). Grounding conceptual knowledge in modality-specific systems. *Trends in Cognitive Sciences, 7*, 84–91.

Binder, J. R., Westbury, C. F., McKiernan, K. A., Possing, E. T., & Medler, D. A. (2005). Distinct brain systems for processing concrete and abstract concepts. *Journal of Cognitive Neuroscience, 17*, 905–917.

Binder, J. R., Desai, R. H., Graves, W. W., & Conant, L. (2009). Where is the semantic system ? A critical review and meta-analysis of 120 functional neuroimaging studies. *Cerebral Cortex, 19*(12), 2767–2796.

Binder, J. R., & Desai, R. H. (2011). The Neurobiology of Semantic Memory. *Trends in Cognitive Sciences, 15*(11), 527–536.

Binkofski, F., Amunts, K., Stephan, K. M., Posse, S., Schormann, T., Freund, H.-J., et al. (2000). Broca's Region Subserves Imagery of Motion: A Combined Cytoarchitectonic and fMRI Study. *Human Brain Mapping, 11*(273–285), 2000.

Bonner, M. F., Vesely, L., Price, C., Anderson, C., Richmond, L., Farag, C., et al. (2009). Reversal of the concreteness effect in semantic dementia. *Cognitive Neuropsychology, 26*, 568–579.

Bookheimer, S. (2002). Functional MRI of language: New approaches to understanding the cortical organization of emantic processing. *Annual Review of Neuroscience, 25*, 151–188.

Borst, G., & Kosslyn, S. M. (2008). Visual mental imagery and visual perception: Structural equivalence revealed by scanning processes. *Memory and Cognition, 36*, 849–862.

Breedin, S. D., Saffran, E. M., & Coslett, H. B. (1994). Reversal of the concreteness effect in a patient with semantic dementia. *Cognitive Neuropsychology, 11*, 617–660.

Bub, D., & Kertesz, A. (1982). Deep agraphia. *Brain and Language, 17*(1), 146–165.

Bush, G., Luu, P., & Posner, M. I. (2000). Cognitive and emotional influences in anterior cingulate cortex. *Trends in Cognitive Sciences, 4*(6), 215–222.

Castelli, F., Frith, C., Happe, F., & Frith, U. (2002). Autism, Asperger Syndrome and brain mechanisms for the attribution of mental states to animated shapes. *Brain, 125*, 1839–1849.

Castelli, F., Happe, F., Frith, U., & Frith, C. (2000). Movement and mind: A functional imaging study of perception and interpretation of complex intentional movement patterns. *NeuroIm-age, 12*, 314–325.

Caramazza, A., Berndt, R. S., Basili, A. G., & Koller, J. J. (1981). Syntactic processing deficits in a case of conduction aphasia. *Brain and Language, 14*, 235–271.

Coltheart, M. (1980). Deep dyslexia: A right-hemisphere hypothesis. In M. Coltheart, K. Patterson, & J. Marshall (Eds.), *Deep dyslexia* (pp. 326–380). London: Routledge & Kegan Paul.

Coltheart, M., Patterson. K., Marshall, J. C. (1987). Deep dyslexia since 1980. M. Coltheart, K. Patterson & J.C. Marshall (Ed.) *Deep dyslexia* (2nd ed.). International library of psychology (pp. 407–451). New York: Routledge (xi, pp. 490 phasia. *Cortex*, 17, 333–348).

Crutch, S. J., Troche, J., Reilly, J., & Ridgway, G. R. (2013). Abstract conceptual feature ratings: the role of emotion, magnitude, and other cognitive domains in the organization of abstract conceptual knowledge. *Frontiers in Human Neuroscience, 7*, 186. doi:10.3389/fnhum.2013.00186

Desai, D. H., Binder, J. R., Conant, L. L., & Seidenberg, M. S. (2010). Activation of Sensory-Motor Areas in Sentence Comprehension. *Cerebral Cortex, 20*, 468–478.

D'Esposito, M., Detre, J. A., Aguirre, G. K., Stallcup, M., Alsop, D., Tippet, L. J., et al. (1997). A functional MRI study of mental image generation. *Neuropsychologia, 35*, 725–730.

Farah, M. J. (1995). The neural bases of mental imagery. In M. S. Gazzaniga (Ed.), *The Cognitive Neurosciences* (pp. 963–975). Cambridge, MA: The MIT Press.

Fiebach, C. J., & Friederici, A. D. (2004). Processing concrete words: fMRI evidence against a specific right-hemisphere involvement. *Neuropsychologia, 42*, 62–70.

Fliessbach, K., Weis, S., Klaver, P., Elger, C. E., & Weber, B. (2006). The effect of word concreteness on recognition memory. *Neuroimage, 32*, 1413–1421.

Friederici, A. D., Opitz, B., & Cramon, D. Y. (2000). Segregating semantic and syntactic aspects of processing in the human brain: An fMRI investigation of different word types. *Cerebral Cortex, 10*, 698–705.

Gallese, V. (2003). The manifold nature of interpersonal relations: the quest for a common mechanism. *Philosophical Transactions of the Royal Society of London. Series B: Biological Sciences, 358*(1431), 517–528.

Ghio, M., Vaghi, M. M. S., & Tettamanti, M. (2013). Fine-Grained Semantic Categorization across the Abstract and Concrete Domains. *PLoS ONE, 8*(6), e67090. doi:10.1371/journal.pone.0067090

Glenberg, A. M., Sato, M., Cattaneo, L., Riggio, L., Palumbo, D., & Buccino, G. (2008). Processing abstract language modulates motor system activity. *The Quarterly Journal of Experimental Psychology, 61*, 905–919.

Goodglass, M., Hydel, M. R., & Blumstein, S. (1969). Frequency, Picturability and Availability of Nouns in Aphasia. *Cortex, 5*(2), 104–119.

Grossman, M., Koenig, P., DeVita, C., Glosser, G., Alsop, D., & Detre, J. (2002). The neural basis for category-specific knowledge: An fMRI study. *Neuroimage, 15*, 936–948.

Halpern, A. R., & Zatorre, R. J. (1999). When that tune runs through your head: A PET investigation of auditory imagery for familiar melodies. *Cerebral Cortex, 9*, 697–704.

Harris, G. J., Chabris, C. F., Clark, J., Urban, T., Aharon, I., Steele, S., et al. (2006). Brain activation during semantic processing in autism spectrum disorders via functional magnetic resonance imaging. *Brain and Cognition, 61*, 54–68.

Hoffman, P., & Lambon Ralph, M. A. (2011). Reverse concreteness effects are not a typical feature of semantic dementia: evidence for the hub-and-spoke model of conceptual representation. *Cerebral Cortex, 21*, 2103–2112.

James, C. T. (1975). The role of semantic information in lexical decisions. *Journal of Experimental Psychology: Human Perception and Performance, 104*(2), 130–136.

Jeannerod, M. (1995). Mental imagery in the motor context. *Neuropsychologia, 33*, 1419–1432.

Jeannerod, M., & Decety, J. (1995). Mental motor imagery: A window into the representational stages of action. *Current Opinion in Neurobiology, 5*, 727–732.

Jeannerod, M. (2001). Neural simulation of action: a unifying mechanism for motor cognition. *NeuroImage, 14*, 103–109

Jessen, F., Heun, R., Erb, M., Granath, D., Klos, U., & Papassotiropoulos, A. (2000). The concreteness effect: Evidence for dual-coding and context availability. *Brain and Language, 74*, 103–112.

Katz, R. B., & Goodglass, H. (1990). Deep dysphasia: Analysis of a rare form of repetition disorder. *Journal of Brain and Language, 39*(1), 153–185.

Kiehl, K. A., Liddle, P. F., Smith, A. M., Mendrek, A., Forster, B. B., & Hare, R. D. (1999). Neural pathways involved in the processing of concrete and abstract words. *Human Brain Mapping, 7*, 225–233.

Kousta, S., Vigliocco, G., Vinson, D. P., Andrews, M., & Del Campo, E. (2011). The representation of abstract words: Why emotion matters. *Journal of Experimental Psychology: General, 140*(1), 14–34.

Kroll, J. F., & Merves, J. S. (1986). Lexical access for concrete and abstract words. *Journal of Experimental Psychology: Learning, Memory, and Cognition, 12*(1), 92–107.

Lane, R. D., Reiman, E. M., & Schwartz, G. E. (1998). Neural correlates of levels of emotional awareness: Evidence of an interaction between emotion and attention in the anterior cingulate cortex. *Journal of Cognitive Neuroscience, 10*(4), 525–535.

Locke, J. (1685). Of abstract and concrete terms. In An essay on human understanding. Retrieved April 15, 2012, from: http://oregonstate.edu/instruct/phl302/texts/locke/locke1/Essay_contents.html

Marschark, M., Richman, C. L., Yuille, J. C., & Hunt, R. R. (1987). The role of imagery in memory: On shared and distinctive information. *Psychological Bulletin, 102*, 28–41.

Martin, N., & Saffran, E. M. (1992). A computational account of deep dysphasia: Evidence from a single case study. *Brain and Language, 43*(2), 240–274.

Mestres-Missè, A., Münte, T. F., & Rodriguez-Fornells, A. (2008). Functional neuroanatomy of contextual acquisition of concrete and abstract words. *Journal of Cognitive Neuroscience, 20*, 2153–2166.

Noppeney, U., & Price, C. J. (2004). Retrieval of abstract semantics. *Neuroimage, 22*, 164–170.

Paivio, A. (1967). Paired-associated learning and free recall of nouns as a function of concreteness, specificity, imagery and meaningfulness. *Psychological Reports, 20*, 239–245.

Paivio, A. (1971). *Imagery and verbal processes*. New York: Holt, Rinehart & Winston.

Paivio, A. (1991). Dual coding theory: Retrospect and current status. *Canadian Journal of Psychology/Revue Canadienne de Psychologie, 45*, 255–287.

Perani, D., Cappa, S. F., Schnur, T., Tettamanti, M., Collina, S., & Rosa, M. M. (1999). The neural correlates of verb and noun processing: An PET study. *Brain, 122*, 2337–2344.

Pexman, P. M., Hargreaves, I. S., Edwards, J. D., Henry, L. C., & Goodyear, B. G. (2007). Neural correlates of concreteness in semantic categorization. *Journal of Cognitive Neuroscience, 19*, 1407–1419.

Reilly, J., Grossman, M., & McCawley, G. (2006). Concreteness effects in lexical processing of semantic dementia. *Brain and Language, 99*, 147–148.

Roeltgen, D. P., Sevush, S., & Heilman, K. (1983). Phonological agraphia Writing by the lexical-semantic route. *Neurology, 33*, 755.

Rüschemeyer, S.-A., Brass, M., & Frederici, A. D. (2007). Comprehending Prehending: Neural Correlates of Processing Verbs with Motor Stems. *Journal of Cognitive Neuroscience, 19*(5), 855–865.

Sabsevitz, D. S., Medler, D. A., Seidenberg, M., & Binder, J. R. (2005). Modulation of the semantic system by word imageability. *Neuroimage, 27*, 188–200.

Saffran, E. M., & Martin, N. (1990). Neuropsychological evidence for lexical involvement in short-term memory. In G. Vallar & T. Shallice (Eds.), *Neuropsychological impairments of short-term memory* (vol. xiii, pp. 145–166, 524 pp). New York: Cambridge University Press.

Sakreida, K., Scorolli, C., Menz, M. M., Heim, S., Borghi, A. M., & Binkofski, F. (2013). Are abstract action words embodied? An fMRI investigation at the interface between language and motor cognition. *Frontiers in Human Neuroscience, 7*, 125.

Shallice, T., & Warrington, E. K. (1975). Word recognition in a phonemic dyslexic patient. *The Quarterly Journal of Experimental Psychology, 27*, 187–199.

Shallice, T., & Cooper, P. C. (2013). Is there a semantic system for abstract words? *Frontiers in Human Neuroscience, 7*, 145.

Schwanenflugel, P. J., Harnishfeger, K. K., & Stowe, R. W. (1988). Context availability and lexical decisions for abstract and concrete words. *Journal of Memory and Language, 27*, 499–520.

Schwanenflugel, P. J. (1991). Why are abstract concepts hard to understand? In P. J. Schwanenflugel (Ed.), *The Psychology of Word Meanings* (pp. 223–250). Hillsdale, NJ: Erlbaum.

Scorolli, C., Binkofski, F., Buccino, G., Nicoletti, R., Riggio, L., & Borghi, A. M. (2011). Abstract and Concrete Sentences, Embodiment, and Languages. *Frontiers in Psychology, 2*, 227.

Scorolli, C., Jacquet, P. O., Binkofski, F., Nicoletti, R., Tessari, A., & Borghi, A. M. (2012). Abstract and concrete phrases processing differentially modulates cortico-spinal excitability. *Brain Research, 1488*, 61–70.

Skipper, L.M., & Olson, I.R. (in press). Semantic Memory: Distinct Neural Representations for Abstractness and Valence. *Brain and Language.*

Strain, E., Patterson, K., Seidenberg, & Mark, S. (1995). Semantic effects in single-word naming. *Journal of Experimental Psychology: Learning, Memory, and Cognition, 21*(5), 1140–1154.

Tettamanti, M., Manenti, R., Rosa, P. A. D., Falini, A., Perani, D., Cappa, S. F., et al. (2008). Negation in the brain: Modulating action representations. *Neuroimage, 43*, 358–367.

Vigliocco, G., Kousta, S., Della Rosa, A. P., Vinson, D. P., Tettamanti, M., Devlin, J. T., Cappa, S.F. (2013). The neural representation of abstract words: The role of emotion. Cerebral Cortex, pp. 1–11.

Vigliocco, G., Meteyard, L., Andrews, M., & Kousta, S. (2009). Toward a theory of semantic representation. *Language and Cognition, 1*(2), 219–247.

Wallentin, M., Østergaard, S., Lund, T. E., Østergaard, L., & Roepstorff, A. (2005). Concrete spatial language: See what I mean? *Brain and Language, 92*, 221–233.

Wang, J., Conder, J. A., Blitzer, D. N., & Shinkareva, S. V. (2010). Neural representation of abstract and concrete concepts: A meta-analysis of neuroimaging studies. *Human Brain Mapping, 21*(10), 1459–1468.

Warrington, E. K. (1975). The selective impairment of semantic memory. *Quarterly Journal of Experimental Psychology, 27*, 635–657.

Weiss, S., & Mueller, H. M. (2013). The non-stop road from concrete to abstract: high concreteness causes the activation of long-range networks. *Frontiers in Human Neuroscience*. doi:10.3389/fnhum.2013.00526.

Whalen, P. J., Bush, G., Mcnally, R. J., Wilhelm, S., Mcinerney, S. C., Jenike, M. A., et al. (1998). The emotional counting stroop paradigm: A functional magnetic resonance imaging probe of the anterior cingulate affective division. *Biological Psychiatry, 44*, 1219–1228.

Whatmough, C., Verret, L., Fung, D., & Chertkow, H. (2004). Common and contrasting areas of activation for abstract and concrete concepts: an H15 2O PET study. *Journal of Cognitive Neuroscience, 16*, 1211–1226.

Wiemer-Hastings, K., Krug, J., & Xu, X. (2001). *Imagery, context availability, contextual constraints and abstractness*. In: Proceedings of the 23rd Annual Meeting of the Cognitive Science Society (pp. 1106–1111). Hillsdale, NJ: Erlbaum.

Wilson-Mendenhall, C.D., Simmons, W.K., Martin, A., & Barsalou, L.W. (2013). Contextual processing of abstract concepts reveals neural representations of non-linguistic semantic content. *Journal of Cognitive Neuroscience*.

Wise, R. J. S., Howard, D., Mummery, C. J., Fletcher, P., Leff, A., & Büchel, C. (2000). Noun imageability and the temporal lobes. *Neuropsychol, 38*, 985–994.

Chapter 6
Language, Languages, and Abstract Concepts

> *Are our own concepts of 'time,' 'space,' and 'matter' given in substantially the same form by experience to all men, or are they in part conditioned by the structure of particular languages?*
>
> Whorf 1939/2000, p. 138

6.1 Introduction

Aim of the present chapter is to present additional evidence favouring the WAT proposal. While in the previous chapter, the focus was on language acquisition, here the focus is on the role linguistic information plays for abstract concepts representation, independently from acquisition. We will present rather sparse evidence, obtained in different domains and research areas, with no pretense of exhaustivity. We will start with the description of a computational linguistic study showing that a rich linguistic context is more relevant for abstract than for concrete concepts; then, we will turn to analysis of sign language indicating that for signs referring to abstract concepts, strategies based on the exploitation of language are used. Larger part of the chapter, however, is dedicated to the review of cross-linguistic studies. The aim of this review is to provide support to the hypothesis that abstract concepts are more influenced by linguistic variability, i.e., that the differences between different languages are more marked for abstract than for concrete concepts.

6.2 Abstract Concepts and Rich Linguistic Context: Computational Linguistics Evidence

One possible way to investigate how abstract and concrete concepts are represented is to ask participants to produce the characteristics of a given concept and then to analyze the relationships between the features produced and the concept itself. We have briefly mentioned some examples of feature generation tasks in Chap. 1 (e.g., Barsalou and Wiemer-Hastings 2005; Roversi et al. 2013). It is generally assumed that this task allows accessing information on how concepts are represented (Wu and Barsalou, 2009; Mcrae et al. 2005). Recent further evidence obtained with a

A. M. Borghi and F. Binkofski, *Words as Social Tools: An Embodied View on Abstract Concepts*, SpringerBriefs in Cognition,
DOI: 10.1007/978-1-4614-9539-0_6, © The Author(s) 2014

free association task reveals that language associations characterize more abstract than concrete concepts, while sensorimotor information characterizes both concrete and abstract concepts (Marques and Nunes 2012). Here, we will briefly focus on a study in which the generated features were analyzed in order to determine the influence of physical and linguistic context in concrete and abstract concepts representation. We will illustrate in detail this study, which was recently conducted by Recchia and Jones (2012) at Indiana University, since we think that its results provide support to the WAT proposal. The authors designed a novel online game to collect norms for more than 500 concepts, both concrete and abstract ones. Participants were required to perform a feature generation task, that is to produce 10 properties to describe a concept; they were told that another participant would have to guess the target-words from their description. Their analysis focused on 3 measures, i.e., number of features (NFs), contextual dispersion (CD), and number of semantic neighbors (NSN). They found that for abstract words, NSN and CD were significant predictors of the performance in lexical decision (a task requiring to distinguish between words and non-words in a given language), but NFs was not. As to concrete words, NFs and CD were significant predictors of latency in lexical decision, but NSN was not. CD was the only measure of semantic richness that significantly predicted the performance on another task, naming, and in this case, there was no difference between abstract and concrete words. As to the features produced, abstract concepts elicited more communicative acts, more evaluations, more social artifacts/actions, and more cognitive states/operations/affects features than concrete words. Concrete concepts, instead, evoked mostly perceptual features, locations (e.g., "helicopter air"), and associated objects. The high frequency of communicative acts characterizing abstract concepts is fully in line with the predictions advanced by WAT, and also the high number of mental states and emotions are compatible with it, for the reasons discussed in Chaps. 1 and 3. However, while the NFs predicted lexical decision times with concrete words, it did not predict them with abstract words.

More crucial for WAT is the finding that NSN is a predictor of lexical decision times of abstract concepts, while NFs is a predictor for concrete ones: In other words, abstract concepts benefit of rich linguistic contexts, while concrete words of rich physical contexts. NSN represents the richness of linguistic contexts in which a given word appears: the relevance of this measure for abstract concepts is predicted by WAT and, more generally, by theories according to which abstract concepts rely more on language than concrete words. Obviously, this might depend on different factors: on the peculiar acquisition modality of abstract words, as hypothesized by WAT, or on the fact that abstract words do not have concrete referents, thus, participants need to rely on linguistic elements to represent them (e.g., Paivio 1986). As the authors themselves recognize, this result is not in conflict with the idea that abstract concepts are grounded in sensorimotor states, but theories according to which both concrete and abstract concepts are grounded in non-linguistic content should be extended to explain this finding. Similarly, theories of abstract concepts that do not consider the importance of linguistic information, as the conceptual metaphor view or other embodied views, are not necessarily disconfirmed by these results but they should be extended to account for this finding.

6.3 Abstract Concepts and Sign Language: Some Examples from Italian Sign Language

Sign languages provide an important source of evidence in support of the WAT view. Here, we will refer more specifically to Italian Sign Language (LIS, Lingua dei Segni Italiana) (Volterra 1987; Capirci et al. 1998), even though the same considerations can be extended to other sign languages (for a more thorough analysis of how examples extracted from LIS can be used to support theories of abstract concepts and words, see Borghi et al., in submission; an important source of information is the Ph.D. dissertation by Gianfreda (2011; see also Gianfreda et al. in press). Evidence favoring the conceptual metaphor theory is easy to find within LIS (for a recent analysis of American Sign Language in which the domain of politeness is analyzed in terms of the conceptual metaphor theory, see Roush 2011): for example, signs such as "to know," "to think," "to understand," and "to remember" refer to the same metaphor, that is to the idea that the head is the container of knowledge, that comprehension consists in grasping something and putting it in the head container and that recall consists in retrieving information from it. The fact that signs the aim of which is to represent through a concrete action an abstract notion make an extensive use of metaphors referring to concrete objects and domains is relatively obvious. Similarly, it is quite intuitive that signs refer to events or situations. The presence of such signs can be used as support of Barsalou and Wiemer-Hasting's view of abstract concepts. For example, the sign used to indicate "December" refers to Christmas, that is to a salient event occurring during that month.

Finding in sign languages supports to the idea that linguistic representations play a major role for abstract concepts and words is, instead, all but straightforward and might seem counterintuitive. Crucially, however, LIS is full of examples of initializations, i.e., of cases in which the hand configuration reproducing the initial letter of the word is used to convey meaning, and other sign languages share this characteristics with it. In particular, American Sign Language is particularly prone to initializations (Olga Capirci, personal communication). Let us start with an example of a polymorphic sign, the sign referring to "communicate," which is similar in LIS and ASL. This sign is polymorphic as it combines a strategy based on initialization with a strategy based on metaphor use (Russo 2005). This sign combines indeed the hand configuration representing the capital letter C with a reciprocal movement of the two hands, possibly due to the underlying metaphor that "interaction is exchanging objects" (Roush 2011). Miscommunication implies a combination of the sign for communicate, followed by a hand drop with a change in orientation, indicating the failure of communication. In LIS, these two signs underwent interesting changes: at first, the sign was made in front of the mouth, and then a bit lower, probably due to the acquired concept that communication cannot be limited to spoken communication, but that it implies also gestural, signed, and more generally bodily communication. What is relevant for the WAT proposal is the use of a linguistic strategy, initialization, even for a sign that can be represented through metaphor use.

More crucial for the WAT view, however, are signs referring to rather "pure" abstract concepts, such as "truth" and "philosophy." In the signs indicating "true" and "truth," a strategy based on initialization is used: speakers form the initial V with the index and middle fingers and move it in front of their face, sometimes reinforcing the affirmative meaning with a forward head movement (see Fig. 6.1).

While LIS does not distinguish between "true" and "truth," in ASL the two notions are represented differently. "True" is represented by using an iconic gesture grounded on the straight-path image schema (Roush 2011): The meaning of "true" is represented through the image of an object sent from the mouth along a straight line. In order to represent "truth," a slight variation is introduced which is relevant for us. The gesture is given by a movement of the index and middle fingers in a straight line on the hand. It is therefore possible that the iconic gesture referring to the straight-path image schema is complemented by a lexicalization—the two fingers probably depict an H, i.e., the H present in the noun "truth."

Other interesting examples of initialization or of language exploitation in LIS are words referring to disciplines. A striking example is given by the sign for "philosophy" (filosofia), which is made using a part of the word that has a semantic meaning. Even if etymologically the word derives from Greek and means "love for knowledge," in Italian the first part of the word "filosofia," namely "filo," means "wire." This is exploited by the sign, which is represented by reproducing a wire moving away from the head of the speaker with a twirling movement. Further examples relevant to our aims are represented by two other nouns referring to scientific disciplines, as linguistics and literature. In the sign for "linguistica" (linguistics), the initial L is mimicked and the hand is moved as if it moved away from the mouth, while in the sign referring to "letteratura" (literature), the initial L again is mimicked, this time as if it moved away from the hand, probably to convey the meaning of (writing) a letter. These two cases are interesting because they combine a strategy based on initialization with a strategy in which a specific body part (mouth, hand) is involved to constrain and delimit the meaning.

Other cases in which initialization is used concern proper or arbitrary names: For example, all days of the week are initialized, that is the first letter of the name is used to refer to the day: L M M G V S D. In contrast, initialization occurs only in one case for the names of the month: to say "ottobre" (October), the letter O is used. For the other months, it is more immediate the reference to a situation or a salient event occurring in that period (e.g., the meaning of December is signed referring to Christmas days, July is represented referring to the harvest). Alternatively, some months are represented using symbols: For example, May is represented as the month of the Madonna; thus, the position of hands which is typical of certain pictorial styles representing Madonna is used. The wide use of initialization for the signs referring to the days of the week but not to the months

Fig. 6.1 An example of initialization in LIS (Lingua dei Segni Italiana): the sign for "truth/true" (verita'/ vero). The signer forms the initial V with the index and middle fingers and moves it in front of his face. In some occasions, the affirmative meaning is reinforced with a forward head movement. From Volterra (1987, p. 73). The sign exemplifies how language can be exploited to represent abstract concepts

suggests that it is a strategy mainly used when other strategies, such as the anchoring of a name to a specific object, event or situation, fail. It is also possible that initialization is widely used for names as those of the days since these words are mostly taught at school; indeed, initialization is a phenomenon linked more to the written than to the spoken language.

We believe that these few examples from Italian Sign Language are very relevant to WAT, as they suggest that in order to represent some abstract concepts language is exploited to better ground the signs. This clearly appears in the wide use of initialization for proper and arbitrary names and for names of disciplines, and for pure abstract names such as "truth," and in the example of the sign for philosophy, in which part of the word, i.e., filo (wire) is used and mimicked to convey the meaning of the overall term.

6.4 Abstract Concepts and Differences Between Languages

One of the tenets of the WAT proposal and one of the stronger hypothesis deriving from it claims that, given that abstract concepts activate more linguistic information compared to concrete concepts, they should be more affected by linguistic variability. In his label feedback hypothesis, Lupyan (e.g., Lupyan 2012) clarifies that it should be important to classify behavior on different tasks as (a) influenced by language; (b) influenced by the different spoken languages; (c) not influenced by language. We will try to show that, compared to concrete concepts, abstract concepts are both more influenced by language and by the different spoken languages.

In support of our claim, we will report examples of cross-linguistic studies on the impact of language on categorization, which indicate that, when the stimulus space is more structured, as in the case of concrete concepts, the influence of linguistic diversity is less marked. For abstract concepts, instead, there is more room for the influence of language, as demonstrated by the fact that different languages differently partition the stimulus space. A similar view was proposed by Gentner and Boroditsky (2001), according to whom the influence of language is more marked in the conceptualization of relations, expressed through verbs and spatial prepositions, than of objects. As demonstrated by Gillette et al. (1999), indeed, objects can be easily identified through observation. As anticipated, Gillette et al. (1999) had adult participants observing videos of mother–child interaction and trying to guess the content of "mystery words" during their talk. While they were able to guess the nouns 45 % of the times, their ability to guess the verbs dropped to only 15 % correct guesses. In addition, they were more able to guess concrete verbs as "push" than abstract ones: mental states verbs such as "think" and "see" were never identified when subjects could rely only on the visual context; rather, their meaning was typically inferred from the syntactic construction used.

To support our claim, we will start with concrete concepts and then refer to progressively more abstract concepts: We will describe studies on concepts of concrete objects, such as containers, then on motion and locomotion verbs, on spatial relations, and then we will turn to studies on abstract entities such as "time" and "number," and finally on abstract verbs such as mental states. One influent study on the relationship between language and categorization in concrete objects was conducted by Malt et al. (1999) who asked Chinese, Spanish, and English speakers to perform two different tasks: a naming and a sorting one. Participants were presented with black and white pictures of 60 containers and were required to label them, as well as to group them into piles on the basis of their physical characteristics, of their function, or of their overall qualities. Results showed a high variability in the naming pattern, indicating that the boundaries of linguistic categories differ substantially across languages. In contrast, the sorting results revealed that the different speakers perceived the categories in a very similar way, as the high correlations between the sorts suggested. These results open the possibility that named categories differ from similarity-based categories. The first need to be more similar within a given language, and have more rigid and fixed boundaries, since speakers have to converge during communication; similarity-based categories instead are not used for communication; thus, they do not need to have explicit boundaries (Sloman et al. 2001). Importantly for us, these results show that the impact of linguistic diversity on a non-linguistic task with a kind of concrete objects, i.e., containers, is limited. This suggests that the representation of containers is not strongly influenced by linguistic diversity, even if these results do not exclude that there is some room for influence of language on categorization. Examples of a dissociation between the naming pattern and the conceptual representation can be found also with verbs referring to motion and locomotion (for a review, see Malt et al. 2010). In general, verbs can be considered to a certain extent as more abstract than concrete objects (Gentner and Boroditsky 2001), but motion and locomotion verbs are clearly grounded in the sensorimotor system and are constrained by biomechanic aspects. English and Spanish motion verbs such as "walk" and "run" differ: English verbs typically encode the manner of movement (e.g., "walk," "run," "stroll"), and the path is encoded through an adverb while Spanish verbs usually encode path or direction of movement (e.g., "entrar," "salir": Mary enters the shop vs. Mary enters into the shop). Participants observed video-clip of events and encoded them either using language or not, and then they performed a recognition memory task and a similarity judgment task. Even if Spanish and English speakers differently encoded the manner and the path of motion, linguistic differences did not influence recognition memory neither in the linguistic nor in the non-linguistic encoding condition (Gennari et al. 2002); however, language influenced the similarity task, even if only in the linguistic condition. The study reveals that conceptual and linguistic categories differ and suggest that the influence of language is present but limited. In a more recent cross-linguistic study, Malt et al. (2008) compared motion and locomotion verbs in English, Japanese, Spanish, and Dutch. They found that two broad categories formed on the basis of biomechanical constraints, "to walk" and "to run," characterize all languages; beyond this distinction, the different languages differently partition the stimulus space (e.g., the English words "jog," "run," and "sprint" correspond to a single Japanese word).

The studies we have briefly overviewed suggest that the influence of language on categorization in concrete domains is limited, as revealed by the dissociation between naming pattern and similarity judgments for objects (containers), and by the fact that different characteristics of motion verbs did not impact memory; however, the results of these studies do not exclude that language impacts categorization, particularly when fine-grained distinctions between motion verbs are considered.

Consider now relations which are typically expressed by spatial preposition. In a variety of studies, Melissa Bowerman and collaborators have demonstrated the effect of language on categorization of spatial categories. For sake of brevity, we will refer here just to one example. While English only distinguishes between containment and support, Korean distinguishes as well between tight containment (e.g., ring on a finger) and loose containment (e.g., apple in a bowl). In a variety of studies, Choi and Bowerman and collaborators (e.g., Choi and Bowerman 1991; Choi et al. 1999; for a review, see Bowerman and Choi 2003) demonstrated that these differences already appear in children's spontaneous speech at 17–20 months and influence the perception of spatial relations later. In addition, habituation and preferential looking paradigms revealed the early sensitivity of English and Korean children to spatial relations such as containment and adherence in comprehension tasks, already during the first year of life, and showed that already at 18–23 months Korean children paid attention to adherence, while English speaker children did not. These results suggest how the developmental pattern of the acquisition of spatial relations might take place: Sensitivities that are not relevant to the spoken language are dropped with time, similarly to what happens in infants for sensitivity to phonetic distinctions. Importantly for us, they suggest an important role played by language in categories referring to relations rather than to concrete objects.

Consider now abstract concepts, such as "time" and "number." The example of time is paradigmatic. A growing number of studies have been conducted to investigate the notion of time, in particular in its relation with the more concrete domain of space. Even if spatial metaphors are used in most languages to refer to time, the specific mapping between space and time differs depending on the language. A growing amount of experiments have demonstrated how tight the relationships between space and time are (for reviews, Bonato et al. 2012; Santiago et al. 2011). We will describe here only some studies, in which the influence of language on the concept of time emerges more clearly. Boroditsky (2001) started from the observation that in English, people typically use front/back terms to talk about time (e.g., the talk of the good times ahead or behind them, they move meetings forward, etc.), while in Mandarin Chinese, people use horizontal but also vertical metaphors to speak about time: earlier times are up, and later times are down. The fact that Chinese speakers use different spatial metaphors for time leads to a different representation of time for Chinese and English speakers, as she demonstrated with a clever priming paradigm. Chinese speakers were faster to confirm that March comes earlier than April if they had just seen vertically displayed pairs of objects or entities (e.g., a black and a white worm/ball); the opposite was true for English speakers. A further experiment with Mandarin–English bilinguals revealed that the advantage of the vertical dimension over the horizontal one was more pronounced if they had learned English late. In addition, Boroditsky demonstrated that if English speakers learn to talk about time as Chinese do, they start to change the way they represent time. This study raised some controversy since in a different study a Chinese researcher, Chen (2007), showed that in Chinese, horizontal metaphors prevail over vertical metaphors. He found it estimating the frequency of usage, focusing on news selected through Google and Yahoo search. Furthermore, in four experiments, the author failed to replicate the priming results obtained by Boroditsky (2001). Even if its results were not replicated, in our view, the study by Boroditsky (2001) is important because to our knowledge, it was one of the first to suggest that in an abstract domain such as that of time, language influences and shapes thought. The future, for example, is represented differently: in English and other languages, such as Italian, the future is represented as ahead from us and the past as behind us, but its representation differs in other languages: for example, in Mandarin Chinese, it is up. In Aymara, an Amerindian language spoken in the Andean of western Bolivia, southeastern Peru, and northern Chile, the mapping is completely reversed: the word for front means also past, and the word back means future. Núñez and Sweetser (2006) conducted an analysis of gestures performed by Spanish and Aymara speakers as well as by Spanish–Aymara bilinguals and found that the different metaphors used in the two languages influence time conceptualization. Casasanto (2008) started from the consideration that in English, the distance metaphor is more frequent than the amount metaphor to refer to time, while the opposite is true for Greek (e.g., a long meeting vs. a large meeting). He reports a study aimed at verifying to what extent people estimations of time were influenced by the ability to evaluate the length of a growing line or the growing quantity of water in a container (for a similar method see also Casasanto and Boroditsky 2008). In keeping with the metaphors adopted in their own languages, time estimates provided by English speakers were influenced by length and not by quantity, while the opposite was true for Greek speakers. An increasing amount of studies we are not going to review here, but which can be relevant for the WAT proposal, suggest that the notion of time is grounded both in language and in the body. Time progression is perceived as going from left to right in certain cultures, from right to left in other cultures, due to conventions linked to the reading/writing direction. We will report just a few examples. Santiago et al. (2007) found that Spanish participants respond faster to words referring to the future on the right and to the past on the left (see also Flumini and Santiago 2013), and Ouellet et al. (2010) demonstrated that Hebrew speakers show a reversed right-to-left mapping (see also Fuhrman and Boroditsky 2007; Sell and Kaschak 2011).

Consider now a further example: abstract verbs. Goddard (2003) demonstrated how the meaning of "thinking" varies consistently across languages. More recently, Goddard (2010) has shown that the majority of words referring to emotions and mental states are language specific, beyond a small set of meanings which are shared by many languages, such as think, feel, want, and know. For example, words such as "sad" and "unhappy" in English do not have a Chinese counterpart, since Chinese does not distinguish between "fatalistic sadness," "confused sadness/malincholy," and "ethical and altruistic grief."

A final example concerns numbers and the ability to use them during counting. As anticipated in Chap. 1, the concept of number is rather idiosyncratic among abstract concepts. Many authors have provided compelling evidence that numbers are grounded and that finger counting represents the basis for number acquisition (for a review, see Fischer and Brugger 2011; Fischer et al. 2012). The literature on numerical cognition is vast and complex, and we are not going to review it here, also due to the specificity of this abstract concept. Here, we focus only on the issue of whether counting is affected by linguistic differences or not (Gelman and Gallistel 2004; Gordon 2004). Gordon (2004) investigated the Piraha culture in the

Brasilian part of Amazonia, characterized by a one-two-many counting system. The absence of a linguistic-based counting system limits the ability of the Piraha people to enumerate exact quantities when exceeding two or three items. While subjects possessing a linguistically based numerical system have an exact sense of numerical quantity, non-numerate participants possess an imprecise and vague notion of number, as revealed by their performance on a variety of tasks, as naming the number of items in a stimulus, constructing sets of equivalent numbers, judging the more numerous among more sets, mentally performing additions and subtractions. Across different tasks, however, Gordon found that the ability to use an analog estimation process was present. Overall, these studies suggest that language might play an important role for the abstract concept of number and for numerical processing abilities. We will not discuss here whether this implies the existence of two different numerical systems: one rather universal on number approximation and another for counting and arithmetic, which is language based, as some authors propose (e.g., Pica et al. 2004). What is relevant for us is only the importance of language for the concept of number. As clearly argued by Gelman and Gallistel (2004, p. 442), "reports of subjects who appear indifferent to exact numerical equality even for small numbers, and who also do not count verbally, add weight to the idea that learning a communicable number notation with exact numerical reference may play a role in the emergence of a fully formed conception of number."

Due to space reasons, we will not discuss the implications of the results we reviewed for the proposal of linguistic determinism, according to which language shapes thought (Whorf 2000/1939, 1956), neither will we review the debate that followed. It is sufficient to say that in the last years, there has been a renaissance of the Whorfian point of view, supported by evidence in a variety of domains. The results we have briefly illustrated, even if they do not support linguistic determinism in its stronger version, can at least be framed within the idea proposed by Slobin (1987, 1996) that thinking and thinking for speaking might differ. According to Slobin, during language processing, attention is directed to the aspects of experience which are encoded in the grammar of a specific language. The review we made suggests at a minimum that language differences affect thinking for speaking. More importantly for the WAT proposal, our review indicates that the impact of language on thinking for speaking is more pronounced for certain domains, as the abstract domain when compared with the concrete one (Boroditsky 2001; Boroditsky and Prinz 2008). Further research is necessary, in order to investigate this important issue.

6.5 Conclusion: Influence of Language on Abstract Concepts

We started the present chapter with a question of Benjamin Lee Whorf: "Are our own concepts of "time," "space," and "matter" given in substantially the same form by experience to all men, or are they in part conditioned by the structure of particular languages? (Whorf 1939/2000, p. 138)." The aim of this chapter was not to review the hot debate on whether thought is determined or influenced by language—we start indeed from the assumption that the influence of language is pervasive (Malt and Wolff 2010), and we do not think this represents a departure from an embodied view since language is a form of experience. The aim of this chapter was to verify to what extent the influence of language differently affects the representation of concrete (e.g., bottle) versus abstract words (e.g., time). From the evidence we reviewed, we believe we can come to two conclusions. First, language plays an important role in the representation of abstract concepts, as suggested by the computational model and by the analysis on sign language. The influence of language on conceptual representation is not in contrast with an embodied approach: according to WAT, all concepts are grounded in the sensorimotor system. But this is not the whole story. We also reviewed evidence showing not only that language influences abstract concepts more than concrete ones, but that different languages differently impact abstract concepts, and that the influence of linguistic diversity is higher in the case of abstract than of concrete words.

In "The Analytical Language of John Wilkins," Borges describes "a certain Chinese Encyclopedia," the Celestial Emporium of Benevolent Knowledge, in which it is written that animals are divided into:

> those that belong to the Emperor, embalmed ones, those that are trained, suckling pigs, mermaids, fabulous ones, stray dogs, those included in the present classification, those that tremble as if they were mad, innumerable ones, those drawn with a very fine camelhair brush, others, those that have just broken a flower vase, those that from a long way off look like flies.

Our review indicates that cultural and linguistic aspects do indeed influence concepts. However, the version we adopt is less extreme than that proposed by Borges: The influence of language on cognition is high for abstract concepts, while it is less important (even if present) for concrete concepts, such as that of animal, since the environment and the body provide a better-defined structure that needs to be shaped by linguistic input to a much lesser extent.

References

Barsalou, L. W., & Wiemer-Hastings, K. (2005). Situating abstract concepts. In D. Pecher & R. Zwaan (Eds.), *Grounding cognition: The role of perception and action in memory, language, and thought* (pp. 129–163). New York: Cambridge University Press.

Bonato, M., Zorzi, M., & Umiltà, C. (2012). When time is space: Evidence for a mental time line. *Neuroscience Biobehavioral Review, 36*(10), 2257–2273.

Boroditsky, L. (2001). Does language shape thought? English and Mandarin speakers' conceptions of time. *Cognitive Psychology, 43*, 1–22.

Boroditsky, L., & Prinz, J. (2008). What thoughts are made of. In G. Semin & E. Smith (Eds.), *Embodied grounding: Social, cognitive, affective, and neuroscientific approaches*. New York: Cambridge University Press.

Bowerman, M., & Choi, S. (2003). Space under construction: Language-specific spatial categorization in first language acquisition. In D. Gentner & S. Goldin-Meadow (Eds.), *Language in mind: Advances in the study of language and thought* (pp. 387–427). Cambridge: MIT Press.

Capirci, O., Cattani, A., Rossini, P., & Volterra, V. (1998). Teaching sign language to hearing children as a possible factor in cognitive enhancement. *Journal of Deaf Studies and Deaf Education, 3*(2), 135–142.

Casasanto, D. (2008). Who's afraid of the big bad Whorf? crosslinguistic differences in temporal language and thought. *Language Learning, 58*, 63–79.

Casasanto, D., & Boroditsky, L. (2008). Time in the mind: Using space to think about time. *Cognition, 106*, 579–593.

Chen, J. Y. (2007). Do Chinese and English speakers think about time differently? Failure to replicate Boroditsky (2001). *Cognition, 104*, 127–136.

Choi, S., & Bowerman, M. (1991). Learning to express motion events in English and Korean: The influence of language-specific lexicalization patterns. *Cognition, 41*, 83–121.

Choi, S., McDonough, L., Bowerman, M., & Mandler, J. M. (1999). Early sensitivity to language-specific spatial categories in English and Korean. *Cognitive Development, 14*, 241–268.

Fischer, M. H., & Brugger, P. (2011). When digits help digits: Spatial–numerical associations point to finger counting as prime example of embodied cognition. *Frontiers in Psychology, 2*, 260. doi:10.3389/fpsyg.2011.00260

Fischer, M. H., Kaufmann, L., & Domahs, F. (2012). Finger counting and numerical cognition. *Frontiers in Psychology, 3*, 108. doi:10.3389/fpsyg.2012.00108

Flumini, A., & Santiago, J. (2013). Time (also) flies from left to right if it is needed! In M. Knauff, M. Pauen, N. Sebanz, & I. Wachmuz (Eds.), In: *Proceedings of the 36th Annual Conference of the Cognitive Science Society* (pp. 2315–2320). Austin, TX: Cognitive Science Society.

Fuhrman, O., & Boroditsky, L. (2007). Mental time-lines follow writing direction: Comparing English and Hebrew speakers. In D. S. McNamara & J. G. Trafton (Eds.), *Proceedings of the 29th Annual Conference of The Cognitive Science Society* (pp. 1001–1007). Austin, TX: Cognitive Science Society.

Gelman, R., & Gallistel, C. R. (2004). Language and the origin of numerical concept. *Science, 306*, 441–443.

Gordon, P. (2004). Numerical cognition without words: Evidence from Amazonia. *Science, 306*, 496–499.

Gennari, S., Sloman, S., Malt, B. C., & Tecumseh Fitch, W. (2002). Motion events in language and cognition. *Cognition, 83*(1), 49–79.

Gentner, D., & Boroditsky, L. (2001). Individuation, relativity and early word learning. In M. Bowerman & S. Levinson (Eds.), *Language acquisition and conceptual development* (pp. 215–256). Cambridge: Cambridge University Press.

Gianfreda, G. (2011). *Analisi conversazionale e indicatori linguistici percettivi e cognitivi nella Lingua dei Segni Italiana (LIS)*. PhD dissertation, University of Macerata.

Gianfreda, G., Volterra, V., & Zuczkowski, A. (in press). L'espressione dell'incertezza nella Lingua dei Segni Italiana (LIS). *Ricerche di pedagogia e didattica.*

Gillette, J., Gleitman, H., Gleitman, L., & Lederer, A. (1999). Human simulations of vocabulary learning. *Cognition, 73*(2), 135–176.

Goddard, C. (2003). Thinking across languages and cultures six dimensions of variations. *Cognitive Linguistics, 14*(2-3), 109–140.

Goddard, C. (2010). Universals and variation in the lexicon of the mental state concepts. In B. C. Malt & P. Wolff (Eds.), *Words and the mind how words capture human experience* (pp. 72–92). Oxford: Oxford University Press.

Lupyan, G. (2012). What do words do? Toward a theory of language-augmented thought. In B. H. Ross (Ed.), *The psychology of learning and motivation,* (Vol. 57, pp. 255–297). New York: Academic Press.

Malt, B., Gennari, S., Imai, M., Ameel, E., Tsuda, N., & Majid, A. (2008). Talking about walking biomechanics and the language of locomotion. *Psychological Science, 19*, 232–240.

Malt, B. C., Sloman, S. A., Gennari, S., Shi, M., & Wang, Y. (1999). Knowing versus naming: Similarity and the linguistic categorization of artifacts. *Journal of Memory and Language, 40*(2), 230–262.

Malt, B. C., & Wolff, P. (2010). *Words and the mind. How words capture new experience.* New York: Oxford University Press.

Malt, B., Gennari, S., & Imai, M. (2010). Lexicalization patterns and the world to words mapping. In B. C. Malt & P. Wolff (Eds.), *Words and the mind. How words capture new experience* (pp. 29–57). New York: Oxford University Press.

Marques, F. J., & Nunes, L. D. (2012). The contribution of language and experience to the representation of abstract and concrete words: Different weights but similar organization. *Memory and Cognition, 40*(8), 1266–1275.

McRae, K., Cree, G. S., Seidenberg, M. S., & McNorgan, C. (2005). Semantic feature production norms for a large set of living and nonliving things. *Behavior Research Methods, 37*, 547–559.

Núñez, R. E., & Sweetser, E. (2006). With the future behind them: Convergent evidence from Aymara language and gesture in the crosslinguistic comparison of spatial construals of time. *Cognitive Science, 30*, 401–450.

Ouellet, M., Santiago, J., Israeli, Z., & Gabay, S. (2010). Is the future the right time? *Experimental Psychology, 57*(4), 308–314.

Pica, P., Lemer, C., Izard, V., & Dehaene, S. (2004). Exact and approximate arithmetic in an amazonian indigene group. *Science, 306*, 499–501.

Paivio, A. (1986). *Mental representations: A dual coding approach.* New York: Oxford University Press.

Recchia, G., & Jones, M. N. (2012). The semantic richness of abstract concepts. *Frontiers in Human Neuroscience, 6*, 315. doi:10.3389/fnhum.2012.00315

Roversi, C., Borghi, A. M., & Tummolini, L. (2013). A marriage is an artefact and not a walk that we take together: An experimental study on the categorization of artefacts. *Review of Philosophy and Psychology, 4*(3), 527–542.

Roush, D. R. (2011). Language between bodies: A cognitive approach to understanding linguistic politeness in American sign language. *Sign Language Studies, 11*(3), 329–374.

Russo, P. (2005). A crosslinguistic, cross-cultural analysis of metaphors. *Sign Language Studies, 5*, 333–359.

Santiago, J., Lupiáñez, J., Pérez, E., & Funes, M. J. (2007). Time (also) flies from left to right. *Psychonomic Bulletin and Review, 14*, 512–516.

Santiago, J., Román, A., & Ouellet, M. (2011). Flexible foundations of abstract thought: A review and a theory. In A. Maass & T. W. Schubert (Eds.), *Spatial dimensions of social thought* (pp. 41–110). Berlin: Mouton de Gruyter.

Sell, A. J., & Kaschak, M. P. (2011). Processing time shifts affects the execution of motor responses. *Brain and Language, 117*, 39–44.

Slobin, D. (1987). Thinking for speaking. In *Proceedings of the Berkeley Linguistic Society, 13*, 435–445.
Slobin, D. (1996). From "thought and language" to "thinking for speaking". In J. Gumperz & S. Levinson (Eds.), *Rethinking linguistic relativity* (pp. 70–96). Cambridge: Cambridge University Press.
Sloman, S. A., Malt, B. C., & Fridman, A. (2001). Categorization versus similarity: The case of container names. In U. Hahn & M. Ramscar (Eds.), Similarity and categorization (pp. 73–86). New York: Oxford University Press.
Volterra, V. (1987, new edition 2004). La lingua Italiana dei segni (LIS). Bologna: Il Mulino.
Whorf, B. (1956). In J. B. Carroll (Ed.), *Language, thought, and reality: Selected writings of Benjamin Lee Whorf*. Cambridge, MA: MIT Press.
Whorf, B. L. (2000). The relation of habitual thought and behavior to language. In J. B. Carroll (Ed.), *Language, thought and reality: Selected writings of Benjamin Lee Whorf* (pp. 134–159). Cambridge, MA: MIT Press. (Original work published 1939).
Wu, L. L., & Barsalou, L. W. (2009). Perceptual simulation in conceptual combination: evidence from property generation. *Acta Psychologica, 132*, 173–189.

Afterword: A Short Story on Abstract Concepts

> I am dominated by one thing, an irresistible, burning attraction towards the abstract.
>
> Gustave Moreau

The capability to abstract is one of the hallmarks of our humanity. In this book, we hope to have shown that explaining the magic of how we can form and use abstract concepts is a complicated but fascinating challenge. And it is a challenge in particular for theories according to which our cognition is grounded and deeply shaped by our body, by its potentialities and by its constraints.

Throughout this book, we have proposed and defended the view that words are social tools and that conceiving words in this way is useful to account for how concepts such as justice, freedom, and democracy are used and represented.

Words are tools because they are material and embodied and because, exactly like physical tools, they extend and augment our cognitive capabilities. But they are a very special and idiosincratic kind of tool. Words are "social" tools because they are public, and also because they extend our capacities allowing us to benefit from the cognitive and physical capacities of other people. Words are social tools because they help us to be immersed in a given cultural milieu. This view on words underlies our proposal on abstract concepts.

In the course of the book, we hope to have presented convincing arguments and evidence favoring the WAT proposal on abstract concepts. As outlined in Chap. 2, the WAT proposal has 5 main tenets: (a) abstract concepts are grounded and embodied, as concrete concepts; (b) language is more crucial for abstract concepts representation, while sensorimotor information is more important for concrete concepts; (c) abstract concepts have a peculiar acquisition modality which ascribes an important role to linguistic and social aspects; (d) abstract concepts activate in the brain more linguistic networks compared to concrete concepts; and (e) abstract concepts representation is more influenced by the differences between languages. We have presented behavioral evidence, obtained both with children and adults, as well as neuroscientific evidence, recorded both with patients and with controls, that supports the WAT view. In addition, we have briefly presented crosslinguistic evidence confirming our tenet 5.

A. M. Borghi and F. Binkofski, *Words as Social Tools: An Embodied View on Abstract Concepts*, SpringerBriefs in Cognition,
DOI: 10.1007/978-1-4614-9539-0, © The Author(s) 2014

As we have seen through the book, most of the ideas presented here do not come out of the blue, but are often widespread in the literature. The idea that abstract words are embodied is shared by many theories, but as we have seen, they differ consistently in the claims they make and in the predictions they formulate. The idea that abstract concepts are represented mainly through the linguistic system is advanced by some theories, but the majority of them do not recognize that abstract concepts are also embodied and grounded and tend to equate language with associations between words, without considering it as an overall experience. In contrast, other theories reduce the role of language, arguing that meaning is captured only through an embodied simulation. The specificity and novelty of WAT consists in stressing the importance of development and of the peculiar acquisition of abstract words. But this is not the whole story. Other views have shown that concrete and abstract words are acquired differently. Further proposals have suggested that linguistic diversity affects more abstract than concrete concepts representation.

But to our knowledge, WAT is the only view that includes all these aspects. It is an embodied theory that ascribes relevance not only to sensorimotor information but also to linguistic experience; it underlies the importance of language for abstract concepts intending language in its complexity and in its social and emotional aspects, not equating meaning with a network of linguistic associations; it is a proposal on words acquisition that considers the bodily effects of a given acquisition modality; it is a view that connects a given acquisition modality with the way in which concepts are represented in the brain and with the way in which words are used and their meanings are represented in different languages.

Obviously, this is not the end of the story. There are a lot of things we have not done in this book. The WAT proposal should be refined in light of novel evidence in different areas. We have spoken of concrete and abstract concepts and word meanings in a general sense, but we have not distinguished between different categories of words. For example, words expressing adverbs and prepositions might be more abstract than concrete nouns, and verbs might be more abstract than nouns. We have not analyzed enough the fine-grained differences between abstract concepts. We believe further research is needed to investigate more in depth the differences rather than the communalities between different kinds of abstract concepts. It is indeed possible that a unitary theory is not adequate and that different proposals might be better suited to explain subsets of abstract concepts. The developmental trajectory we have outlined is very preliminary, and it should be better articulated and rendered more sophisticated and compelling. Similarly, the bodily consequences of a given acquisition modality should be further investigated and deepened.

In sum, this is just the beginning of a short story on abstract concepts. We do really hope that the story will become longer and that it will be enriched by fruitful ideas and by novel evidence. The topic is so exciting and important that it is worth a try.

Index

A
Abstractness, 2–4, 6, 9–12, 14
Acquisition modality, 71, 82, 83, 89
Action, 39, 40, 42, 43, 51, 53, 57, 58, 61–63
Associative learning, 91

C
Categorization, 3, 5, 7
Common and differential representation of abstract and concrete concepts, 7, 9–11, 95–98, 103–105
Concreteness, 7–13
Concreteness effect, 7–11, 95–98, 103–105
Contextual dependency, 7, 8
Crosscultural studies, 111, 116

D
Development, 71, 73, 79, 80, 83, 90

E
Effects of emotional valence, 103, 104
Effects of mental imagery, 97
Embodied cognition, 19, 30, 50, 52, 71, 78, 79, 89, 90
Emotions, 44, 46, 47, 55–57, 64
Explanations, 21, 24, 25, 27, 28, 30–33

G
Grounded cognition, 39, 44, 47, 49–52, 63, 64

H
Hierarchical levels, 5

I
Imageability, 7–10
Inner language, 32, 33

L
Labels, 21, 24–33
Language acquisition, 75, 78
Language learning, 72, 75–77, 89
Linguistic context, 112
Linguistic diversity, 116, 117, 121

M
Metaphor, 39, 47–53
Multiple representation, 51, 53

N
Neuroimaging of abstract and concrete concepts, 97, 102

P
Perceptual strength, 8, 9, 11, 12

R
Reversed concreteness effect, 96, 97, 104, 105

S
Sign language, 111, 113, 115, 121
Situations, 39, 44, 45, 55, 60, 64
Social cognition, 42, 44, 47, 60

W
Word associations, 60–64

A. M. Borghi and F. Binkofski, *Words as Social Tools: An Embodied View on Abstract Concepts*, SpringerBriefs in Cognition,
DOI: 10.1007/978-1-4614-9539-0, © The Author(s) 2014

MIX
Papier aus verantwortungsvollen Quellen
Paper from responsible sources
FSC® C105338

If you have any concerns about our products,
you can contact us on
ProductSafety@springernature.com

In case Publisher is established outside the EU,
the EU authorized representative is:
Springer Nature Customer Service Center GmbH
Europaplatz 3, 69115 Heidelberg, Germany

Printed by Libri Plureos GmbH
in Hamburg, Germany